ECONOMIC ANALYSIS OF AGRARIAN INSTITUTIONS

Economic Analysis of Agrarian Institutions

The Case of Tenancy

Binoy Goswami

With a Foreword by Ramesh Chand

Orient BlackSwan

ECONOMIC ANALYSIS OF AGRARIAN INSTITUTIONS: THE CASE OF TENANCY

ORIENT BLACKSWAN PRIVATE LIMITED

Registered Office
3-6-752 Himayatnagar, Hyderabad 500 029, Telangana, India
e-mail: centraloffice@orientblackswan.com

Other Offices
Bengaluru, Bhopal, Chennai, Guwahati, Hyderabad, Jaipur, Kolkata, Lucknow, Mumbai, New Delhi, Noida, Patna, Vijayawada

ISBN 978-93-5287-090-5

026148

17102017

Typeset in
Sabon Lt Std 10.5/12.5
by Manmohan Kumar, Delhi

Printed in India at
Glorious Printers, Delhi

Published by
Orient Blackswan Private Limited
3-6-752, Himayatnagar Hyderabad 500 029
e-mail: info@orientblackswan.com

Contents

Tables and Figures

Tables

Figures

Abbreviations

AFIC	Area under Fertiliser-Intensive Crops
AWP	Area under Winter Paddy
CAGR	Compound annual growth rates
EXT	Access to Extension
FIN	Access to Finance
FL	Farm Labour
FMCs	Field Management Committees
FS	Farm Size
GCA	Gross cropped area
GSDP	Gross State Domestic Product
HYV	High-Yielding Variety
IR	Extent of Irrigation
LBSNAA	Lal Bahadur Shastri National Academy of Administration
NSS	National Sample Survey
OBC	Other Backward Classes
PHYV	Area under High-yielding Varieties
SC	Scheduled Caste
ST	Scheduled Tribe
VLEW	Village-level extension worker

FOREWORD

Agrarian institutions play a significant role in promoting output growth and income generation and its distribution. One such institution is tenancy, which was the central focus of post-Independence agricultural policy. The general impression that one gets from the relevant literature is that sharecroppers usually undersupply efforts in comparison to fixed-rent tenants, and hence are inefficient. Therefore, tenancy or leasing arrangements have serious implications for agricultural production, productivity, and for the overall agricultural development.

It is an established fact that the land tenure system inherited from the British at the time of independence was neither equitable nor efficient. Consequently, tenancy laws were enacted across the states. The tenancy laws of all the states, passed in the 1960s and 1970s, sought to improve the incentive of tenants to supply adequate effort in cultivation through providing them with security of tenure. In other words, the objective of efficiency was sought to be achieved by making access to and distribution of land more egalitarian.

Although all the states passed tenancy laws, only a few states implemented them seriously. While the tenancy laws were not fully implemented in most states, some provisions in these laws had resulted in certain unwarranted outcomes. Scholars have in fact shown that even in the states where tenancy laws were implemented successfully, problems related to tenancy arrangements have resurfaced in one form or another. Concealed tenancy, shorter duration of the lease contract, and restrictions on occupational mobility in rural areas are some of the unwarranted outcomes. All these outcomes have adverse implications for rural development in general and agricultural development in particular, which have already been discussed by some scholars. Meanwhile, the context in which these laws were formulated has also undergone changes. The characteristics of landowners in contemporary times are remarkably different from those of the landlords at the time when the country became independent. As per the report of the 70th round of the National Sample Survey, marginal and small holdings constituted 85.41

per cent of the total ownership holdings in 2013. In other words, most owners of land and tenants are probably not remarkably different today. These developments point to the fact that the time has come to take a fresh look at the existing tenancy laws, and modify them to adapt to the changing agro-economic realities of the countryside. It is in this context that the present work assumes relevance.

Taking Assam as a basket case, the author reviews the tenancy situation in the state and examines the implications of various forms of tenancy contracts for agricultural production and productivity. Further, effort is also taken to move beyond the conventional literature on the subject and analyse the implications of the tenancy contracts for the sustainable use of agricultural land. This is a valuable addition to the existing literature on the subject.

The main analysis presented in the book is based on primary data that the author generated through an extensive field survey across the state of Assam. This has enabled an appropriate contexualisation of the policy recommendations presented in the book in the ground realities of tenancy relations. The author's field visits allowed him to go beyond the tenancy question, and enabled him to examine the issue of agricultural development in the state from a broader perspective. For example, one recent development that the author has mentioned in his discussion of the current agricultural set-up in the state is the emergence of the rental markets of agricultural capital goods. The author explains how the smooth functioning of these rental markets—which can be enormously beneficial, especially for the small and marginal farmers—is contingent upon the adoption of certain reforms in the existing tenancy laws of the state. Therefore, the book, while addressing the core research issue of the state of tenancy, also makes an attempt to suggest a holistic policy path for the agricultural development of the state. Although the study is based on the state of Assam, the policy recommendations could be valid even for other states, given that tenancy is prevalent across Indian states and is rising. States also need a fresh look at the legal framework for land lease to bring about necessary changes in the law in order to institutionalise concealed and oral tenancy, and facilitate easy lease-in and lease-out by balancing the interests of the lessee and the lessor.

I believe that this book will be a useful reference for anyone with an interest in analysing the tenancy and institutional framework forming India's agrarian set-up.

Professor Ramesh Chand
Member, NITI Aayog
Government of India

Preface

Back in the early twentieth century, Alfred Marshall wrote about the inefficiency of sharecropping relative to the fixed rent tenancy contract. Following Marshall, a surfeit of studies came up which examined whether sharecropping was indeed inefficient. Going one step ahead, some studies investigated the rationale behind the existence of this form of tenancy, despite its perceived inefficiency under different circumstances and geographical contexts. Meanwhile, there were some other studies that sought to answer the question as to whether tenancy in general and sharecropping in particular could be inimical to technological progress and agricultural growth. It appears therefore that issues related to tenancy relations have been studied over time and across space by many scholars. Thus, the question that one might ask is: Why another book on tenancy relations? The answer is that despite a considerable number of works, much of the issues related to tenancy relations have not been conclusively settled yet.

Further, what emerges unequivocally from the existing literature is that the nature of tenancy relations, and therefore their implications, are very context-specific. In other words, there exists the possibility of gaining new insights from a study on tenancy relations in a new context. Moreover, with the increasing concern for sustainable development, the time is now rife to expand the horizon of analysis and enquire about the implication of various forms of the tenancy contract for the sustainable use of agricultural land, and this study does so. Considering Assam as a basket case, this book delves into all the relevant issues related to tenancy relations. In fact, the book goes beyond the institution of tenancy and explores some dimensions of another emerging agrarian institution—the rental markets of capital goods. The study observes that the smooth and efficient functioning of these rental markets, which could be beneficial to all farmers, especially the small and marginal ones, is interconnected with the appropriate management of tenancy relations.

This book is an improved and expanded version of my doctoral work. In the course of completing this work, I have benefited immensely from the expertise and vast knowledge of Professor M. P. Bezbaruah of Gauhati University, under whose supervision I carried out my doctoral work. I shall remain indebted to him for his invaluable guidance and constant inspiration. This book is an outcome of Professor Bezbaruah's advice and encouragement, and I would like to place on record my profound gratitude to him.

Thanks are due to Raju Mandal, Amiya Sarma, Bimal Phookan, Alok Ranjan Dutta, Surajit Saikia, Hiren Sarma, and Minata Devi for the help I received from them at different stages of this work. I thank the district agricultural officers of the districts in which the field study was conducted for helping me with the identification of the villages for collecting data. I am grateful to all the farmers who voluntarily agreed to answer my questions. Without their cooperation, this work would never have been possible. I thank my wife, Anoopa, for reading the first draft of the book and providing me with several critical comments, which undoubtedly helped me to improve upon it. I place on record my appreciation for Roopa Sharma and Proteeti Banerjee of Orient BlackSwan, who have guided me through this book project.

Although the book is based on data from the plains of Assam, it is expected that the work will have relevance for all of India, given that tenancy is widespread in most of the states. I believe that the book will be a useful reference for anybody interested in the institutional aspect of agricultural production. I dedicate this book to my parents (my father, Late Umesh Chandra Goswami, and my mother, Amiya Devi Goswami) for inspiring me to appreciate honest and rigorous academic work.

Binoy Goswami
New Delhi, October 2017

1

Introduction

After the *Green Revolution*, introduced in the mid-1960s, the agriculture sector in India grew impressively, especially in comparison to the period before and immediately after Independence. While during the first 50 years of the twentieth century the average rate of growth of crop output was less than 1 per cent, this increased to 2.4 per cent during 1950–2004. The agricultural growth, impressive as it has been, has however fallen short of targets consistently in spite of the much praised technological improvements and significant investment made in this sector (Vaidyanathan 2010). The sector continues to suffer from stress, which has become quite serious in recent times. This performance of India's agriculture sector raises a most obvious question: If large investments and technological progress are not enough to attain the targets in the agriculture sector, what else is required to sustain the growth of India's agricultural output?

Growth of agricultural output does depend on factors like the adoption of technology, efficient use of agricultural land, access to credit and extension services, and so on. However, it is pertinent to note that the contribution of these factors to agricultural growth can be realised to their fullest potential if, and only if, the agrarian set-up or the institutional organisation within which agricultural production takes place is conducive. Thus, while analysing the growth performance of the agriculture sector, it is pivotal to understand whether the agrarian institutional set-up provides the necessary incentive to apply the factors of production sufficiently.

In practice, agrarian institutions may take different forms, and one of the most important agrarian institutions is that of tenancy. When the ownership of the two most important factors of agricultural production, that is, land and labour, is not uniform across rural households, leasing arrangements that emerge in the form of tenancy contracts can bring about a better matching of these factors. Households that do not own sufficient land relative to their labour can lease-in land from those households that own more land as compared to their labour. The term 'tenancy relations' has many dimensions, encompassing complex historical, social, political, and economic dimensions. However, when viewed through the economic lens, it refers mainly to the tenurial or leasing arrangements of land. Within this definitional scope, the problems and effects of tenancy on agricultural production, class relations, safeguarding the interests of tenants, and so on, are usually considered.

It is an established fact that the agrarian set-up in general, and the land tenure system in particular, which existed in India at the time of Independence were characterised by high levels of inefficiency and exploitation of the tenants. Hence, certain land and tenancy reform measures were introduced after Independence. These reform measures aimed at eliminating inefficiency from the agrarian set-up by establishing an egalitarian land tenure system. Of course, agriculture being a state subject, the enactment of tenancy legislation was left to the states. Given that the states were at different stages of development, these legislations differed in terms of specific provisions, although they all had the same broad objective of making the agrarian set-up efficient and egalitarian. However, these differences became noticeable in terms of the states' implementation of the laws. These laws were never implemented properly by most states, barring a few exceptions. Thus, notwithstanding the successful implementation of tenancy reforms in states like West Bengal and Kerala, not much could be achieved through these legislations in terms of incentivising farmers to eliminate inefficiency from agricultural operations. Nor did the agrarian set-up become more equal. Meanwhile, with the passage of time, many provisions of these laws started becoming largely irrelevant as economic development catalysed changes in the agro-economic realities of the countryside. In fact, as a result of the changes in agro-economic conditions, certain unwarranted outcomes have surfaced in the states where tenancy reforms were implemented (Nair and Menon 2006).

All these developments reaffirm the fact that it is now time to take a fresh look at the issue of tenancy relations, especially its current nature and implications for agrarian development in the context of the changing agro-economic environment of the rural economy. The present study aims to do so by examining the case of the state of Assam in northeast India. It studies the nature of the existing tenancy arrangements in the state and analyses the implications, mainly economic, of such an arrangement for agricultural development.

This chapter provides a critical analysis of three important aspects of tenancy relations, encompassing the existing literature that contextualises this book. Besides, a critical deliberation on the prevailing literature should help us to understand its limitations, and what needs to be done to overcome those limitations.

EFFICIENCY/INEFFICIENCY OF TENANCY CONTRACTS: CONTESTING THEORIES AND CONTRASTING FACTS

Of the two broad forms of tenancy, fixed-rent tenancy is viewed as more efficient than sharecropping in traditional economic literature. Since the fixed rent is in the nature of fixed cost, it does not enter the marginal calculations in the optimisation of the tenant farmer. In choosing his optimal quantity of effort on land, he equates the marginal product of his effort with his marginal cost, and consequently the economic surplus is maximised. In contrast, the sharecropper gets to retain only a part, usually half of what he produces. Hence, in equilibrium he equates half of the marginal product of his effort to his marginal cost and thus stops supplying efforts at a point when the marginal product still exceeds the marginal cost. Therefore, the economic surplus is not maximised. It is in this sense that sharecropping is considered inefficient. In the literature, it is usually referred to as Marshallian inefficiency after Alfred Marshall, who first expounded this phenomenon. This line of argument, however, presumes that the effort of the tenants is unobservable or that the cost of monitoring the tenant's effort is prohibitively high. As opposed to the Marshallian argument, the 'monitoring approach' pioneered by Johnson (1950) asserts that sharecropping can be equally efficient if the landlord does the following: (*i*) stipulate the required intensity of factor use in the lease contract; (*ii*) fund a share of the total costs of cultivation; and (*iii*) lease out land only for a short period. Later, in 1969, Cheung (cited in Bhaumik 1993) provided the proof for Johnson's argument.

The explanation for the contrasting outcomes of the two models can be sought in the assumptions of the models. Contrary to the assumption of the 'Marshallian approach'—the unobservable tenant effort and high monitoring cost—the 'monitoring approach' assumes that supervision of a tenant's effort is economically viable. This approach further assumes that the work decision is taken by the landlords. However, even assuming that the work decision is taken by the tenant, Bardhan and Srinivasan (1971) proved that sharecropping was still an inefficient contract.

Although the Marshallian and monitoring approaches dominate the literature on this issue, they have been criticised by many scholars because of the neo-classical framework along which both models are moulded. A discussion of this aspect can be found in Bell and Zusman (1976). Both models derive their results by assuming that the markets in a rural economy are perfectly competitive. The Marshallian approach assumes that the rental share is determined in a competitive land market by the demand for and supply of leases. But a model formulated by Bardhan and Srinivasan (1971) shows that if an income-maximising tenant demands land, for any rental share less than unity, to lease-in until the marginal productivity of land is zero, it may result in an excess demand for land and allow the landlord to act like a monopolist. The Marshallian approach further assumes that the rental share determined as above has to be higher than the wage rate (which is a tenant's opportunity cost) determined in a competitive labour market. However, in a situation where landownership is highly concentrated and the demand for labour shows strong seasonal variations, the notion that the labour market is competitive and employment offers are available at a perfectly certain wage is difficult to accept (Bell 1977). The imperfection and uncertainty in the labour market make the imputed cost of family labour lower than the market wage rate. One of the consequences of such a phenomenon is the widely discussed inverse relationship between size class and productivity. Thus, it may not be true that sharecroppers of all classes are inefficient. This possibility is missing in the Marshallian approach.

In the Monitoring approach, Cheung (1969) maintains that the income-maximising landlord will design the contract stipulating a minimum input, namely labour intensity, and specify the rental share which has to be higher than the tenant's opportunity cost. Cheung also assumes that the labour supply curve is perfectly elastic. This implies that there are numerous tenants willing to work at the prevailing wage rate. This assumption is required so that the landlord can find some tenant willing to accept the contract designed by him, even if somebody else rejects it. Again, the tenant can refuse the contract offered by a landlord as a perfectly elastic labour supply curve also means the availability of alternative employment opportunities at a perfectly certain wage rate. The tenant would deny the contract when the return from the contract is less than the opportunity cost. Now, if it is true that the tenant can deny a contract, then he should also have the power to influence the design of a contract. Thus, the assumption of a perfectly elastic labour supply ensures that it is not the landlord or the tenant alone who decides the rental share; rather, it is decided through a bargaining process between the two agents. The initial economic position of the agents determines their bargaining power, which in turn changes the character of market participation. Thus, it not always a case of landlord versus tenant; rather, it is a case of the economically powerful versus the weak.

Once it is accepted that the rental share is decided through a bargaining process, Cheung's model loses its validity. The economic status of a tenant depends on his possession of inputs like draught power, managerial skills, etc., besides his own labour. In fact, the landlord would also like to lease out to the economically viable tenant, that is, one who possesses these inputs. However, inputs other than labour which make the tenants viable do not receive formal attention in either model. Problems would not have arisen and Cheung's contract could have been extended to specify the minimum input intensity for these inputs and their rewards; the rewards would have been higher than the respective opportunity cost, had the markets for them been perfectly competitive. However, in reality, markets for these inputs are rarely competitive; in fact, they sometimes do not even exist. When markets are imperfect or non-existent, specifying the rewards above the opportunity cost is impossible. This ultimately makes it impossible for the landlord to enforce a contract specifying the rewards and input intensities.

Thus, it is clear that once the assumption of competitive markets is dropped, both the models will show different outcomes. Another situation in which these models are irrelevant is that of interlocked markets. The interlocking of markets refers to a situation in which the economically powerful party combines a number of contracts, enjoying benefits in the concerned markets simultaneously. This characteristic has an analytical consequence as the functioning of markets cannot be discussed within a competitive framework, not even within the category of market imperfection. In such a situation, it is extremely difficult to disentangle the functioning of the land market from other markets, and the competitive models become grossly inadequate to analyse the efficiency aspect of tenancy contracts (Bharadwaj and Das 1975a).

The Marshallian and the Monitoring approaches have also been criticised because of their ahistorical character. The initial historical situation relating to property relations and the way market power has developed and is being exercised by the more powerful section determine who is taking the decisions concerning the lease, and the terms and conditions attached to it. All of these have implications, as is clear from the above discussion, for the efficiency of a tenancy contract. This point is especially emphasised in the Marxist literature. It can be mentioned here that on the issue of share tenancy contracts, the Marxist have a different stand. Their analysis is based on the view that sharecropping is a mode of production under a semi-feudal agrarian set-up in which the landlords extract surplus from the tenants. They believe that sharecropping, being pre-capitalist in nature, is not suitable for big farmers. Hence, with time, as land gets concentrated in the hands of the big farmers, sharecropping gives way to capitalist farming (Chandra 1974).

The discussion above makes it clear that the theoretical debate on the present issue is inconclusive. Notwithstanding the problems associated with both models, while the Marshallian school of thought suggests that sharecropping is inefficient, the Monitoring approach asserts that there is no reason why sharecropping cannot be equally efficient, provided certain conditions are fulfilled. Like the theoretical debate, the empirical evidence is also not conclusive. Bell (1977), Bharadwaj and Das (1975b), Bhaumik (1993), Dobbs and Foster (1972), Islam and Benerjee (1985), Pant (1983), Narayana and Nair (1994), Shaban (1987), Sharma, et al. (1995), and Tripathy (1985) have found evidence in favour of the Marshallian argument in the Indian context. On the other hand, Chakravarty and Rudra (1973), Chattopadhyay and Sarkar (1997), Chattopadhyay and Sengupta (2001), Dwivedi and Rudra (1973), Junakar (1976), and Rao (1971) have confirmed the results of the Monitoring school. Further, the studies by Chattopadhyay (1979) and Vyas (1970) could draw no decisive result.

Different empirical studies have adopted various methodologies and one cannot disregard the fact that the results of these studies may be influenced by the choice of methodology. For example, Dwivedi and Rudra (1973) compare the performance of tenants and owner-cultivators without taking into account the size classification and find no difference between them. It would, however, be naïve to assume that the performance and behaviour of cultivators across sizes would be the same. However, consideration of size class as an explanatory variable is not the end of the problem. The major problem of most empirical studies is the competitive framework within which they carry out their investigations. As has been discussed, the rural economy is hardly competitive, and drastically different results might appear once the competitive assumption is dropped.

Bell's paper (1977) marks a remarkable departure on methodological grounds from earlier studies while testing the hypothesis that inputs and output per acre on sharecropped holdings will be lower than those on owner-operated holdings of the same fertility. Bell takes care of the problem of imperfection in rural markets and its implications for the efficiency of different tenure forms. To incorporate the impacts of imperfections in rural markets, he considered the differences in the input intensities and output per acre on the leased-in land and own land of the same farmer. He found that the cropping intensity, intermediate input and hired labour intensities and output per acre are higher on owned land than they are on the leased-in land of the owner-tenant. His findings suggest that the tenants were very successful in diverting resources to the land that they own. This implies that sharecropping is less efficient than owner operation, as suggested by the Marshallian line of thought, and thus refutes the argument of the monitoring school. Other studies like Shaban (1987) and Bhaumik (1993), who have adopted the same methodology as Bell, have also found the same sorts of evidence, thereby making a strong case for the Marshallian school of thought.

Why Does Sharecropping Exist Despite its Apparent Inefficiency?

Despite its apparent inefficiency, sharecropping is, however, widely prevalent in the real world. Therefore, it is clear that there must be some factors which compensate for the inefficiency involved in sharecropping. Economists have talked about several such factors and the important ones are discussed below.

Risk and Sharecropping

The rationale behind the existence of sharecropping can be traced to uncertainty in agriculture, which does not figure in the Marshallian world of certainty. Fixed rent places the entire risk of crop failure on the tenant. But sharecropping emerges as a way to share not only the output, but also the risk associated with it by varying the rent payable with the size of the harvest (Stiglitz 1974). Hence, a sharecropping contract is preferred by the tenants under certain circumstances. Besides, assuming the landlord to be risk neutral, it can be shown that even the landlord will prefer sharecropping to fixed rent if the share of the tenant can be reduced to leave him with a higher share. Stiglitz has provided another explanation as to why the landlord might find sharecropping contracts convenient under certain circumstances. This line of thought argues that the tenant's exposure to risk can be reduced by designing a wage-labour contract according to which the tenant will be paid a fixed wage equivalent to his expected return from sharecropping (this is because the tenant will not accept a wage-labour contract if his expected return from sharecropping is more than the fixed wage). But the problem with the wage-labour contract is that it places the entire risk on the landlord. Hence, a risk-averse landlord may not prefer a wage-labour contract.

Another problem associated with the wage-labour contract is that of hidden action or moral hazard arising out of information asymmetry with regard to the skill of the tenant. This can be viewed as a classic case of the principal-agent problem. The tenant may not put in the required effort if his incentives to supply effort are weaker. Hence, to ensure the required effort from the tenant, the landlord will have to monitor the supply of efforts. Monitoring involves costs and these will be very high when lands are scattered and if the landlord is an absentee one. In fact the landlord, especially an absentee one, may be able to monitor only the output and not the inputs supplied by the tenant. In this context, Stiglitz (2004: 34) points out that 'the input of the worker could not be observed, but only his output, and his output was not perfectly correlated with his input.' Hence, a landlord cannot make a tenant liable for a bad harvest. Consequent to all these problems associated with the wage-labour contract, a landlord might not design such a contract. Rather, he would prefer to share the crops with the tenants. Thus, under such circumstances it appears that sharecropping is the most suitable contract for the tenant, and under certain conditions, for the landlord too (Ray 1998).

Ray (1998) has pointed out an objection to the risk-sharing argument for sharecropping. This argument asserts that both landlord and tenant may be better-off by diversifying the resources between fixed rent and wage-labour contract, and that hence, sharecropping should not exist. The landlord can lease out a part of his land for fixed rent to earn a secure income and cultivate the rest through hired wage labour, which gives higher expected returns but places the entire risk on himself. Similarly, the tenants may work as employed wage labour for some part of their time to earn a minimum secure income while the rest of the time can be invested on land leased-in on a fixed-rent basis, taking the entire risk for the latter on themselves. There are, however, several counter-objections to this criticism of the risk-sharing argument for sharecropping. First, fixed-wage contracts have their own incentive problems (which we have already mentioned above), and hence it is not clear why the combination of fixed-wage contracts and fixed-rent contracts should dominate sharecropping. Second, a combination of these two contracts might be practically impossible to accomplish. During the harvest season, when timing is of utmost importance, a tenant may not prefer a wage-labour contract, since he would like to work on his leased-in or own land. Third, in the presence of imperfection in the labour market where the wage rate is uncertain, a wage-labour contract may not be very attractive (Newbery 1977). In such cases, it is ultimately sharecropping which dominates the other forms of contracts.

Double Incentive Problem

There may be cases where both the landlord and the tenant are required to apply effort. But if they have a fixed-rent contract where the tenant gets to retain the entire marginal product, the landlord has no incentive to put in any effort. On the other hand, if the contract is in the form of wage labour, the tenant has no incentive to apply effort as the entire marginal product goes to the landlord. Thus, the Marshallian argument of inefficiency arising from the absence of incentive applies in both directions. In such cases, sharecropping emerges as a compromise solution to this double incentive problem (Ray 1998).

Sharing the Cost of Inputs

As mentioned above, under sharecropping without sharing of cost, the sharecropper gets to retain only half of what he produces, but has to bear the entire cost of production. In equilibrium, he equates half the marginal product of his effort to his marginal cost and thus stops supplying efforts at a point when the marginal product still exceeds the marginal cost. Thus, economic surplus does not get maximised and production remains inefficient. With cost sharing, the marginal cost faced by the tenant is also half. Thus, efficiency under a cost-sharing arrangement is attained as half of the marginal product is equated to half of the marginal cost. Thus, sharecropping may be a preferred contract when the cost is shared by the tenant and the landlord, especially if the inputs used are contractible and their use is observable (Ray 1998).

Limited Liability and Sharecropping

An argument provided by Basu (2005) not only explains the existence of sharecropping, but also establishes it as an efficient contractual arrangement in the event of limited liability. The limited liability axiom asserts that if individual *i* has some financial commitment towards *j* but happens to be bankrupt, then *j* has to forgo his claim (ibid.). The presence of limited liability introduces a certain tension between the two agents (Stiglitz and Weiss 1981). In the presence of limited liability, the tenant would prefer risky projects whereas the landlord would act as a risk-averse person, even if they are innately risk-neutral agents. Share tenancy enables the landlord to influence the tenant's choice behaviour vis-à-vis alternative risky projects more easily and in the direction the landlord prefers.

Sharecropping and Long-Term Co-Operative Relation

A sharecropping contract may often be characterised by the highly personalised and long-term co-operative relationships between the tenant and landlord. The landlord not only receives a share of the output, but also shares a part of the cost of production, besides giving credit to the tenant for production and consumption purposes. Moreover, the landlord helps the tenant in case of contingencies and uses his influence and connection to solve the tenant's problems with other people. The tenant reciprocates with the loyal service of himself and his family, including voluntary domestic help during festive occasions (Hayami 2003: 300). This kind of relationship, commonly termed as patron–client relationship, is a substitute for a set of specialised markets for labour, land, credit, and insurance (Bardhan 1980), which may be beneficial for both tenant and landlord. A landless tenant who finds it extremely difficult to raise credit in the presence of capital market imperfection can receive the required amount of credit from the landlord. On his part, the landlord can avoid the problem of adverse selection arising from information asymmetry with regard to the quality of the worker, since experience from past transactions provides him with the necessary information which is otherwise difficult to come by at the marketplace, and even from monitoring the work of labour since variations in output depend on many factors other than quality of labour.

The co-operative relationship between tenants and landlords is solidified within the total community relationship. In a small community where everybody knows everybody else, the cost of a dishonest act is very high for both parties. This is because a rumour about a tenant / landlord breaching his contract with the landlord / tenant not only endangers his present relations with the landlord / tenant, but also eliminates the possibility of his entering into contracts with other parties in the same community. Thus, the apparent inefficiency of sharecropping can be avoided through co-operative relationships between tenants and landlords, to the advantage of both parties (Hayami and Otsuka 1993).

Thus, it appears from the discussion above that the existence of sharecropping is context-specific. Sharecropping is a diverse phenomenon and a single theory cannot explain the reason for its existence.

Is Sharecropping Inimical to Technical Change and Agrarian Growth?

The debate on whether tenancy contracts can impede technical change and therefore agrarian growth was initiated by Bhaduri (1973). According to Bhaduri, a semi-feudal production relation between landlord and tenant inhibits innovation in agriculture. In this type of relation, the landlord usually assumes the role of moneylender as well, and resists the introduction of improved methods of production. Innovation is not encouraged by the landlord because it might improve the income of the tenant, which in turn will help him to reduce his indebtedness to the landlord. As a result, the landlord would lose the income that he could have otherwise earned by lending to the tenant.

Bhaduri's explanation, when placed in the context of India's 'Green Revolution', however, finds no support. As observed by Byres (1972), the small peasants and the sharecropper could not adopt the new technology (that is, the package of HYV seeds, irrigation, fertiliser, and pesticides) due to a lack of resources and acceptable collateral on which they could get institutional credit. Thus, contrary to Bhaduri's argument, evidence suggests that innovation would require the tenant to increase their indebtedness to the landlord, rather than reducing it. Besides, the semi-feudalism thesis cannot explain why owner-cultivators who hold the major portion of land in the ex-zamindari areas of eastern India do not expand output rapidly (Vaidyanathan 1986).

Newbery (1975) has commented that Bhaduri's explanation is logically inconsistent as the landlord who could resist innovation should also have the power to extract most of the profits resulting from such innovation. He further added that even if the landlord does not have the freedom to devise a suitable contract so as to extract profits from innovation, he can exercise his monopoly power in other markets to compensate for that loss. For instance, the landlord can charge an exploitative rate of interest on the past loan; he could insist that the tenant sell his produce at a price well below the market price; and so on.

Having disagreed with Bhaduri, Newbery (1975) offered the following theory of tenurial impediments to innovation. According to Newbery, if innovation leads to the replacement of an old technique by a more complex one, which requires new and sophisticated skills, and if it is difficult to establish ex-post that the replacement has really taken place, it might create a moral hazard on the part of the tenant. In such a situation, it might be impossible to enforce a contract which specifies the supply of inputs and the sharecropper might tend to under-supply. Thus, if innovation leads to moral hazard, the factors (risk aversion, uncertainty in the labour market, etc.) which make share contract the preferred contract would impede innovations. In such a case, a landlord would also resist innovation if he knew that the tenant would not apply the inputs efficiently, and hence profits could not be realised easily. A wage-labour contract is no better than sharecropping since this would also involve the problem of moral hazard. In a mixed contract, however, a landlord can provide the tenant with the necessary incentives to use the inputs efficiently, or to accept the new technique by raising the fixed rent component and reducing the share rent. But this will increase the tenant's risk and hence might be rejected in favour of the old technique. On the other hand, a large and less risk-averse farmer with a fixed rent contract will find the innovation attractive.

Thus, what transpires from the discussion above is that while the literature relating to tenancy has delved into certain important issues and debated them substantially, these debates are yet to be settled conclusively. Moreover—and most importantly—the existing literature suffers from many limitations. For example, on the issue of the relative efficiency of tenancy contracts, the major and common shortcoming that both the Marshallian and Monitoring schools of thought suffer from relates to the competitive framework within which the models have been moulded. While the markets for agricultural inputs and their services are hardly perfect, both schools of thought derive their results within a competitive framework. The theoretical literature as well as empirical findings of many earlier studies need to be interpreted carefully as they suffer from the methodological flaws discussed above. Insofar as the continuance of sharecropping, despite its apparent inefficiency, is concerned, it appears from the literature that sharecropping is a diverse phenomenon that may arise out of several factors. The appearance or continuance of this contract is contingent upon the nature of the rural economy under study. Hence, a single theory cannot explain all aspects of share tenancy, thereby leaving scope for further exploration. Similarly, further assessment is required on whether sharecropping may impede technical change and, therefore, agrarian growth, as the existing literature fails to establish the findings unambiguously.

Another shortcoming of the existing literature is its limited scope. The concerns of the existing studies are mainly confined to the efficiency implications of tenancy contracts. None of the studies go beyond this and comment on the sustainability implications of these contracts. Given the growing concern for sustainability, the time is now ripe to broaden the debate to encompass the question of whether different forms of tenancy contracts have implications for the conservation of soil productivity as well.

In view of the limitations of the existing literature, the present work, besides verifying the three issues identified from this literature, extends the discussion to examine whether the institution of tenancy has implications for the sustainable use of land. Moreover, while examining the relative efficiency/inefficiency of tenancy contracts, the study considers such parameters that allow one to look at the efficiency/inefficiency debate from a broader perspective, as compared to the narrow focus that the existing literature has brought to bear on this matter.

As mentioned earlier, the study has been conducted in Assam, the most prominent state in northeast India. Viewing Assam as a basket case, the present work seeks a larger understanding of how the agricultural institution of tenancy has had an impact on agricultural productivity and the sustainable use of land. Although the agriculture sector of Assam has been extensively studied, not many studies have dealt with agrarian issues like tenancy elaborately, in spite of its widespread prevalence. This makes the selection of Assam as a case study more meaningful.[1]

Outline of the Book

This study has been organised into seven chapters. Chapter 2 traces the evolution of tenancy relations in the Indian context, as well as in the context of Assam. An overview of the agrarian system with a focus on the incidence of tenancy in Assam as extracted from secondary data has been presented in Chapter 3. Chapter 4 discusses the tenancy situation in the Assam plains, which emerged from inputs gathered through field investigation. The impacts of various forms of tenancy contracts on productivity-enhancing practices and input intensities, and the implications of various tenancy contracts for the sustainable use of land have been analysed in Chapter 5. Further insights into the contemporary agro-economic environment of Assam, gathered during field investigation, have been presented in Chapter 6. The concluding chapter summarises the findings of the study and discusses the policy implications of these findings.

Note

1. The questions raised in this work have relevance for Assam on two counts. First, agriculture is still a dominant sector in terms of its contribution to the Gross State Domestic Product (GSDP) and the share of workers engaged in the sector as well. More than 50 per cent of the state's workforce was employed in agriculture and the sector contributed a quarter of the GSDP in 2009–10 (Government of Assam 2012). Second, the cropping pattern in the state is mainly paddy-oriented and in paddy cultivation, tenancy, especially sharecropping, is widespread (Bezbaruah 1994; Gautam 1995; Kuri 2003; Unit for Land Reform of the LBSNAA 1994).

2

Tenancy Relations in India: Historical Perspective*

How did the institution of tenancy in its present form come to exist in India? To answer this question, one has to look at tenancy relations from a historical perspective since it has its legacy in colonial rule in India. This chapter traces the evolution of tenancy relations in India during British rule and the subsequent developments it witnessed post-Independence.

Tenancy Relations during British Rule

The Land Tenure System during British Rule

Prior to British rule, the agrarian structure in India was characterised by production relations that were self-possessing, self-working and self-sufficient (Mukherjee 1957, cited in Sharma 1995). The situation, however, started changing towards the end of the Mughal Empire. The East India Company got zamindari rights over the villages of Calcutta, Gobindpur, and Sutanuti, and appointed its own foreign zamindar. The Company was concerned only with the maximisation of revenue collection and deployed many methods towards that end. Meanwhile, frequent famines in the later part of the eighteenth century crippled the agrarian economy of India. The revenue collection of the East India Company declined drastically. Thus, with a view to improving revenue collection, Lord Cornwallis introduced the Permanent Settlement or zamindari system in 1793 in Bengal. Under this system, the zamindars became the proprietors of land. Thus, through the Permanent Settlement system, the British rulers introduced the idea of private property

*Portions of this chapter were first published in DIALOGUE 15 (3), Jaunuary-June 2014.

rights. The zamindars were made responsible for collecting and paying a fixed amount of revenue to the Company. Contrary to the expectations of the British rulers, however, this system did not serve their interest. Besides, it inflicted a lot of harm on the rural economy. The zamindars indulged in sub-letting and rack renting, rather than showing any interest in agricultural development. Instead of investing in agriculture, they indulged in conspicuous consumption with the excessive rents collected from the tenants. On the other hand, the tenants had no incentive to supply sufficient efforts in agriculture as they had to surrender everything to the zamindars after retaining only the subsistence output with them. The tenants had no bargaining power to improve their share as they could at any time be evicted by the landlords.

Upon realising that the Permanent Settlement system could not fulfil their objective, the British introduced the Ryotwari system, initially in Madras in 1772, and later extended to Bombay. This system was considered a relatively better arrangement, under which the cultivator was the owner of the land and was responsible for the payment of revenue. Thus, the layer of intermediaries was sought to be abolished. The peasants under this system could not be ejected so long as they paid the fixed rent to the government. However, with the passage of time the Ryotwari system also deteriorated and became very repressive, as the rent to be paid by the tenants was revised upwards many times. Besides this, sub-letting became rampant under this system as it had under the zamindari system. Consequently, agriculture continued to languish under this system too.

Another land tenure system that prevailed in the country at that time was the Mahalwari system, introduced first in Agra and Avadh, and later on in Punjab. Under this system, the entire village was made responsible for the contribution of revenue. Initially, the government used to collect as much as 83 per cent of the gross rental of the estate as revenue, which was later reduced to around 60 per cent.

Thus, the Permanent Settlement system, Ryotwari Settlement and Mahalwari Settlement are the three types of land tenure systems that came to exist during British rule in India. While the Permanent Settlement system had the highest share (57 per cent) of the total privately owned agricultural land under it, only 5 per cent of such areas were under Mahalwari tenure. The remaining 38 per cent area was under the Ryotwari settlement (NCA 1976, Vol. XV, cited in Sharma 1995).

From the above discussion, it is clear that all the land tenure systems of the colonial period were characterised by the exploitation of tenants, in terms of mounting rents and insecurity of tenure, and no investments were made by the landlords for agricultural development. All of this ultimately culminated in a highly inefficient mode of agricultural production. Besides these, there were certain other pitfalls of the British land tenure system. Even though the introduction of private property rights in land facilitated the operation of the land and credit markets, it ultimately resulted in the large-scale transfer of land from poor tenants to rich moneylenders. Upon default, moneylenders used to snatch away the land which was many a time pledged to them by poor tenants borrowing money. Such coercive transfer of land and purchase of land by moneylenders and merchants consequent to the increase in the value of land (due to population pressure and infrastructural development) resulted in a highly skewed distribution of land. The fallouts of such skewed land distribution were the emergence of exploitative tenancy arrangements and a distinct class of agricultural labourers.

Tenancy Situation in India before Independence

At the time of Independence, the agricultural working population numbered 111 million, of which only 4 million (3.60 per cent) were rent receivers and as many as 79 million (71.10 per cent) were landless. These landless people included, among others, the tenants, tenants at will, and the sharecroppers. These three categories accounted for 33.30 per cent of the total agricultural working population (Patel 1952, cited in Sharma 1995). The preponderance of landless people shows the stark divide in the distribution of landholding.

The magnitude and types of tenancy varied significantly across provinces of India on the eve of Independence. In provinces where the zamindari and Ryotwari systems were prevalent, tenants cultivated about 75 per cent of the agricultural area. Modes of tenurial arrangement, however, were different in different places. Sub-tenants cultivated about one-third of the area under the Ryotwari mode in Bombay and Madras provinces. In Tanjore, the leasing arrangement was mostly in terms of sharecropping (Sharma 1995). In Bombay, the landlords used to lease out land to tenants for short periods of time, usually for one year. Tenants had to pay half of the produce as rent. In Gujarat, 30 per cent of the total land under the landlord (locally known as talukdar) was cultivated under leasing arrangements (Fukazawa 1982). In the United Provinces, tenants had hereditary and occupancy rights. In Punjab, there were two types of tenants—occupancy tenants and tenants at will. Occupancy tenants had permanent and heritable rights on land. But besides paying land revenue to the state, tenants had to pay rent to the owner of the land as well. In Bengal, there were three types of tenants: raiyats, under-raiyats, and bargadars. Raiyats were more or less like the occupancy tenants in Punjab. They used to sub-let land to the under-raiyats, who did not have security of tenure. The other category, that is, bargadars, was not even given the status of tenants, let alone security of tenure.

Tenancy Legislations in the Pre-Independence Era

The Bengal Rent Act of 1859 was the first legal attempt to define landlord-tenant relations, keeping in view the ubiquitous discontent and unrest among the peasant class. The Act made some attempts to safeguard the interests of the tenants, especially those of the occupancy raiyats. However, it soon became clear that the Act was not adequate to make a real impact. Consequently, the Bengal Tenancy Act came into place in 1885. This Act was further modified in 1928 and 1938. Some other notable tenancy legislations of that time were (*i*) the Madras Estate Acquisition Act, 1908, which provided the right to transfer land and security of tenure to raiyats, so long as they paid rent; (*ii*) the Orissa Tenancy Act, modelled on the lines of the Bengal Tenancy Act of 1885; and (*iii*) the United Provinces Tenancy Act of 1938, which consolidated the Agra Province Act of 1881 and the Avadh Act of 1886, amended in 1926.

These acts conferred occupancy rights on hereditary tenants. In Ryotwari areas where no tenants existed in government records, no attempt was made to govern landlord-tenant relations until the enactment of the Bombay Tenancy Act of 1939 (Sharma 1995).

LAND AND TENANCY REFORM MEASURES AFTER INDEPENDENCE

As can be understood from the preceding discussion, the agrarian set-up in general and the land tenure system in particular that prevailed at the time of Independence was not conducive to the development of agriculture. There was a very high incidence of tenancy. The landlords were never interested in the development of agriculture, and exploitation of tenants by the landlords was rampant. All the tenancy arrangements of that time were oral and eviction at will predominated. Although some measures were taken before Independence to safeguard the interests of tenants, they failed to have any significant impact. Hence, after Independence the Indian National Congress (INC)-led government undertook certain land and tenancy reform measures. The land reform policy in general and tenancy reform in particular in India, initiated after Independence, had two specific objectives: first, to remove all impediments inherited from the past agrarian structure so as to create conditions under which to raise efficiency and productivity in agricultural production to a higher level. The second objective was to deal with the issues of social injustice and inequality within the agrarian system (Government of India 1961).

Besides economic considerations, the INC also had political obligations to initiate the land reform process. To galvanise the support of the masses during the freedom struggle, the leadership of the INC had promised to bring about changes in the agrarian set-up if British rule could be thrown out. Therefore, after Independence, the government was obligated to put land reform measures in place. In its 45th Karachi session in March 1931, the INC recommended that land revenue and rent paid by the tenants should be reduced substantially. Further, in 1937, the INC formulated an elaborate agrarian programme which contained recommendations that included, among others, the abolition of intermediaries, security of tenure, and reduction of rent (Borgohain 1992). In 1949, the Agrarian Reforms Committee was set up, headed by J. C. Kumarappa. The recommendations of this Committee set the guidelines for the land policy of successive Congress governments. The Committee recommended that (*i*) all intermediary interests should be abolished and land should belong to the tillers; (*ii*) the leasing of land should be prevented, with exceptions for minors, widows, and other disabled persons; (*iii*) continuous cultivation for six years should be the criterion for conferring occupancy right; and (*iv*) tenants should be given the right to purchase land at a reasonable price, to be determined by the land tribunal (Sharma 1995).

The land reform programme in India had four broad components: abolition of intermediaries; ceiling on land holdings; consolidation of land holdings; and tenancy reform.

The abolition of intermediaries is generally agreed to be the one component of land reforms that had been relatively successful (Ghatak and Roy 2007). It started in a real sense in 1948 with the enactment of the legislation in Madras Presidency, which was followed by similar legislations in all the other states. The second component, that is, ceiling on land holdings, sought to distribute surplus land among the landless. The performance in this regard, however, was very poor. According to Misra and Puri (2000), out of the total cultivated area, only 1.7 per cent had been declared as surplus, and only 1 per cent of that had been distributed. Ghatak and Roy (2007: 252) have attributed this poor performance to the following:

> Landowners resisted the implementation of these reforms by directly using their political clout and also by using various methods of evasion and coercion, which included registering their own land under names of different relatives to bypass the ceiling, shuffling tenants around different plots of land so that they would not acquire incumbency rights as stipulated in the tenancy law and possibly even outright eviction.

Another component of the land reform programme was the consolidation of land holdings, which refers to uniting small parcels of land belonging to the same farmer, but situated in distant places in order to raise viability and productivity. However, implementation of this programme was constrained by variations in land quality across plots, and hence basically remained on paper and was never properly implemented. The final component was tenancy reform. The purpose of tenancy reform was to regulate certain aspects of tenancy relations, as opposed to the outright transfer of land under land reform. Tenancy reform in India basically included (*i*) providing security of tenure to the tenants cultivating land continuously for a specific period of time; (*ii*) the regulation of rent to a reasonable level, usually 20–25 per cent of the gross produce; and (*iii*) conferring of ownership rights on the tenants, subject to certain restrictions. Given the socio-economic conditions of small and marginal landowners, the interests of these landowners were also sought to be protected while implementing the tenancy reform measures.

An Assessment of Tenancy Reform Programmes in India

Agriculture being a state subject, all the states after Independence passed their respective tenancy legislations. As the states were at different levels of economic and political development, the nature of state tenancy legislations varied widely. However, all states had the three above-mentioned objectives in common.

THE OVERALL ASSESSMENT

Although all the states passed the tenancy legislations, most of them lacked the political will to implement tenancy reform measures properly. Besides, these laws had many loopholes. Hence, it is not surprising that the tenancy reform programmes in India could barely accomplish their objectives. An overall assessment of tenancy reform measures in India with respect to the aforementioned objectives reveals a very disappointing picture.

Insofar as the first objective is concerned, although a substantial proportion of tenants acquired security, there were large numbers who remained unprotected (Chandra, et al. 1999). With respect to the second objective, the rents to be paid by tenants to the landlords, fixed by the state legislations, varied across states. In some states, the rent was much higher than had been recommended in the Five-Year plans. Again, under the pretext of personal cultivation and voluntary surrender, the landlords evicted tenants on a large scale. Hence, the objective of conferring ownership rights also met with limited success. Most importantly, as tenancy was oral or informal in most cases, all the reform measures remained only on paper, without much effect.

Appu (1975: 1) summarised the status of the implementation of tenancy reform programmes in India thus:

> Even after two decades of tenancy reform, the position of tenants—particularly of the sharecroppers—continues to be precarious in several parts of the country. Insecure tenures have not merely resulted in the perpetuation of social and economic injustice; they have also turned out to be formidable stumbling blocks in the path of the modernization of Indian agriculture. High priority should, therefore, be given to the plugging of loopholes in the existing tenancy laws and the better implementation of the enacted laws.

The situation has not improved even today. In fact, many unwarranted outcomes have surfaced consequent to the enactment of tenancy laws, with many restrictive provisions which went unnoticed for several decades after Independence.

State-Specific Experiences: The Cases of West Bengal and Kerala

While most states failed to implement tenancy legislations properly or lacked the political will, the tenancy reform experiences of two states received much acclaim. Although not free from shortcomings, the tenancy reform experiences of West Bengal and Kerala were hailed as successful, at least at the time that they were implemented.

OPERATION 'BARGA'

Operation Barga itself was not a tenancy reform measure. The Left Front, on coming to power in West Bengal in 1977, launched a programme called Operation Barga. The objective of this progrmme was to implement the hitherto ineffective tenancy laws which sought to regulate rents and provide security of tenure to sharecroppers. A campaign was launched under the programme to help and encourage sharecroppers to register with the Department of Land Revenue of the Government of West Bengal. The registered sharecroppers would then have permanent and inheritable tenure on the leased-in land, provided they paid the legal share of the crop to the landlords as rent. The provisions for security of tenure and regulation of rents were present in the tenancy laws of almost all the states. The only difference between West Bengal and the others was that while in the former the government implemented the laws rigorously, in other states the political will to implement them was missing.

Theoretically, as Banerjee, et al. (2002) have shown, the impact of a measure or programme like Operation Barga on agricultural productivity can be divided into two effects: (*i*) bargaining power effect, and (*ii*) security of tenure effect. The bargaining power effect comes from the fact that after the implementation of the programme, the tenant's bargaining power vis-à-vis the landlord with respect to the share of output increases. The tenant may settle for a higher crop share, which may provide them with incentives to put in greater efforts. Increased supply of efforts may ultimately result in higher productivity or greater efficiency. Security of tenure may impact agricultural productivity from two opposing directions. While on the one hand the threat of eviction may be used by the landlords to induce tenants to supply adequate effort, on the other hand banning of eviction or, alternatively, security of tenure would encourage tenants to put in the required effort, as the tenants become the virtual owners of the land. Which effect dominates is, however, an empirical question. Again, on the equity ground, while banning of eviction would increase the welfare of the incumbent tenants, getting land on lease would become increasingly difficult for potential tenants. Thus, intra-generational equity may be attained at the cost of inter-generational equity (Ray 1998).

Like the theoretical debate, empirical evidence on the impacts of Operation Barga on productivity is also not conclusive. While some studies have shown that Operation Barga has resulted in increased productivity, others have concluded otherwise. Banerjee, et al. (2002) have shown that Operation Barga resulted in productivity improvement by 28 per cent. Shaban (1987) analysed farm-level data from eight Indian villages and estimated that controlling for land quality changes, the evolution of a contractual status of a farm from sharecropper-cultivated to owner-cultivated would increase productivity by 16 per cent. In contrast, Place and Otsuka (2001) are of the opinion that Operation Barga had a depressing effect on productivity because the bargadars lacked entrepreneurial skills and supporting facilities. According to them, security of tenure need not necessarily result in increasing investment in land and greater land use efficiency. Haque (2001), meanwhile, has shown that the belief that tenancy rights would enable tenants to access institutional credit has not been borne out.

Thus, in summary, the impact of Operation Barga on agricultural productivity, both theoretically and empirically, is not clear. Besides, there is a possibility that such programmes may hurt inter-generational equity in terms of tenants' access to land. This implies that tenancy reform programmes like Operation Barga cannot provide a permanent or at least a long-term solution.

Full Transfer of Property Rights through a Ban on Tenancy

The Kerala Land Reform Act (1969), which came into effect from 1 January 1970, vested in governments all the rights, titles and interests of the landowners and intermediaries over the holdings held by the cultivating tenants (Nair and Menon 2006). The Act envisages conferring security of tenure and allows the compulsory transfer of ownership rights to all tenants, including sharecroppers. Thus, there was full transfer or redistribution of property rights in favour of tenants, and they became the owners of the land. Besides this, the Act prohibited the creation of future tenancy and made it illegal. There was no exemption, not even for defence personnel. Thus, land redistribution in Kerala was primarily via the abolition of tenancy (Herring 1980).

Since 1970, 37 per cent of the net sown area has been transferred to 1.3 million former tenants, most of whom are small farmers (Nair and Menon 2006). However, 64 per cent of the transferred area went to the relatively big farmers (Herring 1983). Thus, the effect of tenancy abolition in Kerala has not been conducive to social justice, contrary to popular belief. A study by the Indian School of Social Sciences (1976) pointed out that a small section of tenants who were already better-off obtained ownership rights by purchasing the lands they had leased-in, while a large number of poor tenants were evicted on both legal and illegal grounds. Thus, the benefits of land reforms accrued only to the rich tenants. Moreover, the small farmers who leased out to medium and big farmers lost their ownership rights.

A few independent studies show that consequent to the ban on tenancy, concealed tenancy surfaced, which made the law irrelevant (Nair and Menon 2006; Oommen 1971). In cases where tenants happened to be small or marginal farmers or landless labourers, concealed tenancy was forced upon them. Landlords would often change tenants every year so that the tenancy would not be registered, and the tenants would not get the ownership rights. Besides, the big landlords made use of the loopholes in the tenancy reform legislation to evade the ceiling law. They conferred the tenancy rights of their surplus land to some of their poor relatives, friends, and farm servants, although practically, such lands continued to belong to them. In other words, this was simply a new form of concealed tenancy (Haque and Sirohi 1986).

What transpires from the discussion on the tenancy reforms experiences of West Bengal and Kerala is that while the tenancy reforms programmes in these two states might have achieved their objectives to a large extent, such programmes cannot provide a permanent or long-term solution. These programmes might have been very useful during the time of their formulation; however, given the fact that many unwarranted outcomes had surfaced in both states consequent to the implementation of these programmes, the experiences of West Bengal and Kerala cannot be regarded as long-term solutions to the complex issue of tenancy arrangement. At this point it must, however, be recognised that whether or not the examples of West Bengal and Kerala are viable, the lesson that one can learn from the experiences of these two states is that political will and detailed records of land are essential to implementing a land or tenancy reforms programme. In both states, the government implemented the reform measures vigorously and laid emphasis on tenants registering with the relevant state institutions. Accordingly, the tenants who registered with them received the benefits of tenancy reforms (NCAP 1995–96).

Contemporary Discourse on Tenancy Reform in India: Liberalisation of the Land Lease Market

While the tenancy laws were never implemented in true spirit except in a few states, many unwarranted outcomes surfaced consequent to the ban on tenancy or formulation of many restrictive provisions in these laws. Such undesired outcomes surfaced not only in the states where these laws were implemented, like West Bengal and Kerala, but also in other states. These undesired outcomes, however, went unnoticed for many decades after Independence. Till the mid-1990s, planners remained oblivious to the adverse impacts of the restrictive provisions of tenancy laws of the states, and hence adhered to the existing provisions.

One of these unwarranted outcomes that emerged from the ban on tenancy—or the very stringent conditions laid down with regard to tenancy in the existing tenancy laws of states—was the emergence of concealed tenancy. The Eighth Plan stated that tenancy reforms had not achieved the desired results as the incidence of informal, oral, or concealed tenancies was very high. The 10th Plan stated the following:

> Several states have either banned tenancy completely or have imposed such restrictive conditions that land leases are virtually impossible. Studies by the Lal Bahadur Shastri National Academy of Administration indicate that this has only resulted in concealed tenancy. The ban on tenancy, which was meant to protect tenants, has only ended up hurting the economic interests of the tenants as they are not even recognised as tenants. As a result, they are denied the benefits of laws that provide security of tenure and regulate rent. (10th Five-Year Plan document, Vol. 2: 301)

Besides concealed tenancy, the restrictive tenancy laws had resulted in the under-utilisation of agricultural resources. Fearful of losing the ownership of their land, landlords do not lease out. They either stick to agriculture even if it is not viable, or prefer to keep their land fallow. As a result, the supply of land in the land lease market is less, which restricts the access of tenants to land. Hence, the objectives of land and tenancy reform, that is, to promote efficiency in agricultural production and equity in terms of access to land, could not be achieved to a significant extent. Therefore, it has been recognised that banning tenancy is not an achievable solution, nor is it a desirable one in view of the mismatch in the factor markets. Moreover, the situation in the countryside today is not the same as it was before. There is evidence to show that lessors in many parts of India today are different from those at the time of Independence, many of whom had no interest in agriculture (Sharma 2006).

Thus, in view of the adverse impacts of the earlier provisions of tenancy reforms and the resulting inefficiency in agriculture and changing realities of the countryside, the 11th Plan called for a revision of the existing tenancy laws. The 11th Plan suggested that while security of tenure was necessary to provide producers with the incentive for investment and for enhancing productivity, it should not be confused with ownership rights. To protect the interests of tenants and landowners and also increase agricultural productivity, the following reforms in tenancy legislation were suggested:

a) Tenancy should be legalized in a 'limited' manner. It should provide security to the tenant for the contractual period, which could be long enough to encourage long-term investment by the tenant. It should also protect the rights to the land of the land-owner so that he has an incentive to lease his land instead of keeping it fallow or underutilizing it. Long-term tenure arrangements should thus maximize agricultural production and increase the returns to the farmer, the landlord, and the tenant.
b) Instead of prescribed rentals, which are violated in informal tenancies, an upper and lower bound of rents may be prescribed at the State level. If these bands are wide enough, this will do away with the need for illegal arrangements, ensure that the rents are determined by market forces within the prescribed band, and thus increase efficiency and co-operation of both the willing parties.
c) Legalizing of tenancy within the above framework will result in increasing the supply of land and will encourage all categories

of rural households to participate in the lease market based upon resource endowment, education, employment prospects, prevailing wage levels, and the institutional backup available.

d) As agrarian conditions vary across the States, a one size fit-all prescription cannot be advocated. In cases where the landlords are dominant and there is strong likelihood that interests of tenants may not be safeguarded, special clauses could be necessary.
e) Small land-owners who would otherwise have to operate small uneconomic holdings should have the opportunity to legally lease out land to other farmers with the assurance of being able to resume possession at the end of the stated period of tenancy.
f) The marginal and small landowners should be assisted with adequate institutional support and rural development schemes, so that they are not compelled to lease out land to big farmers or corporate houses, thereby creating conditions for involuntary reverse tenancy. In the case of sharecroppers, they should have access to credit, once they enter into long-term contracts. (Planning Commission, 11th Plan document, Vol. 3: 33)

Thus, the change in the strategy to achieve the objectives of land and tenancy reform policy, that is, to raise efficiency in production and bring about equity in access to land, is clear. In the earlier years of planning, it was suggested that all states take measures through the strict implementation of tenancy laws to bring about equality in access to landholding, eliminate the exploitation of tenants, and thereby improve the welfare of the tenants. Notwithstanding the importance of achieving equity in income and landholdings and the welfare of tenants, the recent plan, in view of the adverse impacts of the existing tenancy laws and the changed realities of the countryside, has, however, called for a relaxation of tenancy laws or liberalisation of the land lease market.

LAND AND TENANCY REFORMS IN ASSAM

Management of Land during Ahom and Colonial Rules

Not much information is available on the land tenure system during the pre-Ahom period in Assam. The little information that is available suggests that the state had been the supreme owner of all lands during this period. During this time, the kings used to make land grants to Brahmin scholars, priests, and religious institutions, a practice that continued even during the period of Ahom rule between 1228–1826 (Guha 2015). In fact, when the king donated land to these privileged sections, a number of people attached to these lands came to work on them. Such an arrangement was made to promote settled cultivation.

During the Ahom regime, the king had ownership over all lands. The king, as the head of the community, distributed the lands for *sali* paddy cultivation uniformly among the *paik*s (the adult male population other than the slaves).[1] In return, the paiks were obliged to offer three to four months' service in a year to the king. A paik could acquire more than the fixed area allotted to him out of surplus wet or sali paddy land, for which he had to pay a nominal revenue in cash, towards the later period of Ahom rule. After the death of a paik or after he reached an age when he could no longer cultivate, the community would take control of the wet land allotted to him. On the other hand, the dry lands could be freely accessed by all for collecting fuel-wood, grazing, and for temporary cultivation. Thus, it becomes evident that a paik had only use right on cultivable land during Ahom rule. However, hereditary private property rights were applicable on homesteads and gardens. On the other hand, the king made unhesitant donations of land to temples, priests, and charitable institutions. The lands thus donated were known as *la-khiraj* grants, and the beneficiaries of such grants did not have to pay revenue to the king.

After the annexation of Assam in 1826, the British brought about some significant changes in the land management system that had prevailed during Ahom rule. Two such major changes were: (*i*) the introduction of the Ryotwari system; and (*ii*) a large part of the erstwhile revenue-free land was brought under the tax net. These changes were introduced to facilitate greater revenue collection.

Since the zamindari system had already been discredited in Bengal, the same system was not put in place in Assam.[2] Instead, the Ryotwari system, under which peasants had permanent, heritable, and transferable occupancy rights on land, was introduced.[3] It was thought that independence of the ryots or peasants would promote an interest in cultivation. In the initial years of British rule, land was provided to the ryot on a short-term lease, mostly on annual lease and in some cases up to five years. The consequence of the short-term lease was that the ryots did not have sufficient incentive to develop and cultivate the land efficiently. Besides, there was widespread exploitation of the ryots by the officers appointed by the government on a short-term basis to collect revenue. Realising the unwarranted effects of a short-term lease, the duration of lease was extended to 10 years under the Settlement Rules of 1970, although annual leases continued to be substantial in number. Again, during 1902–12, the decennial lease was replaced by 20-year leases (Guha 2015).[4]

The other important change was that the government brought under its scrutiny all the lands that had been granted by the Ahom king. A large part of the revenue-free land held by the administrative class under Ahom rule was taken over by the government or sold off for pending rents. Only a few such holders of land could manage to keep the land. However, most of the grants (la-khiraj lands) to Brahmins and religious institutions remained beyond the purview of land revenue and continued to be revenue-free. Only some such grants were brought under the revenue net, and half of the existing revenue rate was charged on them. Such lands came to be known as *nisf-khiraj*. Thus, the *la-khirajdar* and the *nisf-khirajdar* emerged as the main categories of big landholders during British rule. Besides these two groups, there were two other categories of big landholders—Khatdars and Chamuadars. The Khatdars and Chamuadars, however, had to pay full rent. Besides the la-khirajdar, another group of people who received special treatment from the British government was the owners of tea estates. This group of people purchased large areas of land in upper Assam. A majority of them did not have to pay land revenue and had rights over the other resources on their lands. Only a small percentage of tea-estate owners paid land revenue at a concessional rate. The zamindars of Goalpara district and Karimgang division of Cachar district also had the same type of rights as the owners of tea estates and the holders of la-khiraj land.

By the end of the nineteenth century, the entire area under cultivation could be broadly classified into areas under ordinary cultivation and those under special cultivation, that is, tea plantations (Saikia 2014). Both these areas and their further categorisations are shown in Table 2.1. While the area under ordinary cultivation was 76.8 per cent of the total area, the remaining 23.2 per cent was under tea cultivation.

Table 2.1. Break-up of Areas under Ordinary and Special Cultivation in Terms of Revenue Arrangement in 1897–98

Types of Land under Ordinary Cultivation	*Percentage Share in Total Cultivable Area*
Land on which full rate of rent was levied, of which:	
(i) With ryots	61.20
(ii) With planters	4.00
Land on which half rate of rent was levied	8.20
Revenue-free land held by Brahmins and religious institutions	3.40
Total land under ordinary cultivation	76.80
Types of land under special cultivation	
Revenue-free land	13.40
Land on which low concessional rate was levied	9.80
Total land under special cultivation	23.20

Source: Adapted from Guha 2015.

Tenancy during British Rule

At the time of the British annexation of Assam, a large number of tenants were working in the existing estates of the Brahmins and the temples. Many slaves attached to the privileged land grantees of Ahom rule were slowing becoming tenants-at-will. The civil war of 1770–1806 and the Burmese incursions expedited the transformation process. During British rule, the incidence of tenancy further increased, in spite of there being sufficient land for cultivation. Guha (2015) has pointed out the following reasons for this increase in the incidence of tenancy during colonial rule. First, with the expansion in the administrative apparatus, the class of government servants who moved to the newly developed towns became absentee landlords.[5] They had money and thus, could pay rents and hold the leases in their hands. This group of people required tenants to cultivate their land. Second, middlemen like mauzadars, many of whom had acquired land through unscrupulous means, also required tenants to cultivate their land. Third, liberated slaves and the disposed indebted peasants preferred to become tenants. Fourth, there were many ryots who transferred their leases fraudulently to influential middlemen in order to avoid harassment from tax collectors; in the course of time, they were reduced to the status of tenants. Fifth, the settlement of ex-tea garden workers on the wastelands of planters and other landholders also increased the incidence of tenancy. Finally, a section of the peasant class attached to the Brahmins and temples wanted to remain tenants instead of becoming independent ryots in the hope of receiving protection against all contingencies from their landlords. Moreover, while there were abundant lands, those lands were not available in a condition wherein one could start cultivation immediately. Cleaning up the wastelands itself was an investment which the peasants could not afford on their own.

Originally, tenants used to pay rent to landlords in kind. However, once the economy was monetised by the British, the landlords started accepting the rent in cash.[6] Cash rent was particularly preferred by the absentee landlords. Lack of space to store paddy was another reason for accepting rent in cash. The incidence of sharecropping was negligible, and in fact was present only in the case of wet paddy lands in highly populated areas (Guha 2015).[7] The cash rent rate to be paid by the tenant was usually not more than the government rate to be paid by the ryot. This implies that only the la-khirajdar could retain the entire rent received from the tenants, and the nisf-khirajdar could retain a part of it. Besides the rent, the tenants had to make extra payments in terms of various cesses, in addition to providing labour services for a certain number of days a year. As far as the *adhi* or sharecropping was concerned, no extra payment in addition to the stipulated share of produce was required to be made. Payment of government revenue was, of course, the responsibility of the landlords. There used to be variations in the arrangement of sharecropping based on the fertility of land and the extent of participation of tenants and landlords in the cultivation, although the burden of rent under all forms of sharecropping was the same as in the case of cash rent.

Although initially the rent rate was equivalent to the government rate, with the increase in paddy price and population, the demand for good land as well as the rent rate increased. In densely populated areas, the landlords started demanding a rent rate that was two to five times higher than the government revenue rate. Added to the misery of the exorbitant rent rate was the fact that the tenants of big landlords had no occupancy and transfer rights.

Reforms in Landholding and Tenancy Relations

At the time of Independence, there were three categories of people who held lands: the big landholders,[8] the landholders or the long-term lease holders, and the settlement holders or short-term lease holders. Except for the last category, the other two could sub-let lands. In this context, Das (1986) had mentioned that big landholders leased out their lands virtually to the last square foot. A large number of landholders in Brahmaputra Valley as well as in Cachar also sub-let their lands. The rates of rent to be realised from tenants, the period of tenure for which they could enjoy tenancy, and the safeguards against arbitrary ejection were determined at the will of the landlords. According to him, the worst feature of Assam's land tenure system was that a very large area—about 20 per cent of the total settled area—was under annual lease. Thus, in spite of the introduction of the Ryotwari system in Assam (except in Goalpara and Cachar), the land tenure system that emerged through colonial rule was characterised by substantial inequality in landholding, a higher incidence of tenancy, and large-scale exploitation of tenants. Consequently, the peasant class lacked sufficient interest in cultivation and ordinary/peasant cultivation remained inefficient. Thus, reforms in landholdings and tenancy relations became imminent.

As in other parts of India, the euphoria surrounding land reforms touched Assam as well after Independence. Consequently, a number of legislations were enacted towards that end. The Assam State Acquisition of Zamindari Act was passed in 1951 to abolish intermediaries, absentee landlordism, and rack-renting of the tillers. This Act was applicable in the permanently settled areas of Assam and brought a large number of tenants in direct contract with the state. However, certain loopholes, like allowing the erstwhile zamindars and tenure holders to possess large areas of land as private land, had the effect of perpetuating intermediary rights in land even after the formal abolition of the zamindari system (Goswami 1986). Again, through the Assam State Acquisition of Lands Belonging to Religious and Charitable Institutions of Public Nature Act, 1959, the state acquired all rights and interests in lands belonging to Mathas, Satras, and other such institutions.

The Assam Fixation of Ceiling on Land Holdings Act was put in place in 1956 to ensure a more equitable distribution of cultivable land. The Act was further amended in 1975. According to Goswami (1986), acquisition of ceiling surplus land was much below the original estimates. Implementation of the Act was delayed as it was challenged in court. Meanwhile, benami transfer of land took place on a large scale. In fact, acquisition of ceiling surplus land occurred after 1972 only when the ceiling limit was reduced to 50 bighas. In 1961, the Assam Consolidation of Holdings Act was enacted, which sought to consolidate and prevent the fragmentation of holdings below 5 bighas to ensure better cultivation.

The Assam Gramdan Act, 1961 provided for the donation of land by way of Gramdan and the declaration of a village as a gramdan village. Again, the Assam Bhoodan Act, enforced in 1966, provided for the acceptance of individual donation of lands and the distribution and settlement of such lands.

Tenancy Reform

The Goalpara Tenancy Act, 1929 marked a milestone in the history of land reform in Assam. This Act initially prevailed only in the permanently settled areas of the state, covering Goalpara district and Karimgang subdivision of Cachar district. The Act defined the landlord-tenant relationship in this area and aimed at improving the condition of the tenants. Its broad features were: (*i*) occupancy raiyats should be conferred upon the permanent, heritable, and transfer rights; (*ii*) sub-tenants should be provided the rights of use and occupancy; (*iii*) protection should be provided to tenants against illegal eviction and enhancement of land rent. This Act was effective even after the abolition of the zamindari system in 1956–57. It was amended in 1970 to incorporate the provisions of the Adiar Tenant Protection Act, 1948. Finally, it was scrapped in 1974 when The Assam (Temporary Settled Areas) Tenancy Act, 1971 was extended to this hitherto permanently settled area.

In the rest of the state, that is, in areas other than the permanently settled area, the Assam Temporarily Settled Districts Tenancy Act, 1935 was in force. This Act classified tenants into four categories: privileged raiyat, occupancy raiyat, non-occupancy, and under-raiyat. The Act was amended in 1953 and permanent, heritable, and transferable rights were accorded to the privileged and occupancy raiyats. However, the other two categories of tenants were only given the rights of use and occupancy, with protection against illegal eviction.

Another act, the Assam Adiar Protection and Regulation Act, was enacted in 1948. This Act strived to provide protection to tenants against illegal eviction and to regulate the rents to be paid to landlords in the form of share of crop. According to this Act, the tenants were entitled to retain 3/4th of the gross produce provided the landlord supplied the plough cattle, or else 4/5th of the produce.

To improve upon the existing situation, The Assam (Temporary Settled Areas) Tenancy Act came into force in 1971, applicable in the entire state. Even today, tenancy relations in Assam are governed under the purview of this Act. The salient features of the Act are:

(*a*) Types of tenants: The Act divides the tenants into two categories: (*i*) occupancy tenants, and (*ii*) non-occupancy tenants, and prohibits the creation of a new under-tenant tenancy. A person who has held land continuously for three years shall have the right of occupancy in that land. An occupancy tenant has permanent, heritable, and transferable right of use and occupancy in the land of his holding. Any occupancy tenant personally cultivating the land of his tenancy can acquire ownership rights through a written application to the deputy commissioner and then paying the compensation (50 times the full rate of the annual land revenue) determined by the authority. On the other hand, a non-occupancy tenant has the right of possession till he is lawfully ejected and subject to the other provisions of the Act or any customs. Neither occupancy nor non-occupancy tenants can sub-let his land. (Sections 17, Ch. I, Chs II–VI)

(*b*) Rent: The maximum rate of rent payable by an occupancy or non-occupancy tenant is determined as follows:

(*i*) In case of cash rent, not exceeding 3 times of the land revenue payable for such land.

(*ii*) In case of crop rent, 1/5th of the produce of the principal crop. In case of natural calamities or any other grounds when the tenant cannot pay the stipulated amount, a sum equal to double of the annual land revenue should be fair rent.

Rents to be paid by a tenant can be enhanced on the following grounds:

(*i*) If the productive power of the land increases due to fluvial action or any improvement of the land at the expense of the landlords, and

(*ii*) If the land revenue to be paid by the landlord to the government has increased.

Rents can be reduced when the opposites of the above two happen. (Ch. VII)

(*c*) Grounds of ejectment: An occupancy tenant can be ejected only when he uses the land in a manner which renders it unfit for the purpose of the tenancy. A non-occupancy tenant cannot be ejected, except on the following grounds:

'He uses the land in a manner which renders it unfit for the purpose of the tenancy; he has broken a condition of his tenancy consistent with the provisions of this act; he has failed to pay the arrear of rent and if the land is bona fide required by the landlord for his personal cultivation. If the tenant has less than 10 bighas of land then he shall not be ejected on this ground. Again, if the landlord does not cultivate the land personally within one year of the date of ejection of the tenant then the land shall be restored to the tenant's possession'. (Section 50, Ch. IX)

(*d*) Voluntary surrender: No tenant can voluntarily surrender without prior permission of the deputy commissioner, and any voluntary surrender shall not be valid if the tenant does not give at least 3 months' notice in writing to the landlord. Besides, for such surrender of land by the tenant, he has to take the consent and approval of the under-raiyat, if there is any. Such voluntarily surrendered land will not be in possession of the landlords. The deputy commissioner may allot that land to a landless agriculturalist, after which he shall become a non-occupancy tenant of the landlord. (Section 63, Ch. XI)

Like the tenancy laws of other states in India, the Assam (Temporary Settled Areas) Tenancy Act, 1971 has many loopholes (Borgohain 1992). Many scholars have already discussed them in detail. Further, many studies have pointed out that the existing law has not been implemented properly. For example, Gautam (1995) reported that the available legislative measures were weakly implemented only to germinate feelings of insecurity of tenure among tenants. The present study has also assessed the impact of the existing law and examined whether the provisions in the law have resulted in unwarranted outcomes (discussed in Chapters 4 and 5).

NOTES

1. At the time of the establishment of Ahom rule in Assam, the indigenous tribal population used to cultivate only dry fruits. The Ahom migrants introduced the cultivation of *sali* paddy and, in the process, settled cultivation was established to a large extent (Guha 2015).

2. While the Ryotwari system was prevalent in all other parts of the state, the zamindari system was followed in Goalpara district and in Karimgang. Goalpara was initially under the Koch king and then came under the Mughal emperor. When the British acquired Diwani from the Mughals in Bengal, Goalpara also came under the rule of the Company and the zamindari system was introduced here.

3. It was, however, only under the Assam Land and Revenue Regulations of 1886 that the rights of the occupants were defined properly.

4. The long-term lease was offered on wet paddy land, homestead, and garden. On the other hand, annual lease was offered on the dry land. Both long-term and short-term leases were reassessed and renewed at the end of the lease period. Those who were granted short-term leases were known as settlement holders, and the long-term holders were known as land holders. Those to whom the land holders leased out land were known as tenants.

5. Another section of absentee landlords who had no land of their own leased in land from big landlords, and then sub-let it. Many big khiraj landholders also used to lease out land (Saikia 2014).

6. By 1940, the entire economy of Assam had been monetised by the British.

7. The lower incidence of sharecropping during early colonial rule, as documented in some scholarly works and in official statistics even in 1951, has been contested by some scholars. It is true that the incidence of sharecropping was low in the ryotwari districts at the beginning of the nineteenth century, and was confined basically to areas adjacent to the newly developed towns which the absentee landlords had migrated to. However, between 1931–51, there was a marked increase in the number of sharecroppers, especially in Kamrup and Darrang districts. Yet, official statistics show a lower incidence of sharecropping as there were discrepancies in the reporting of sharecropping. Many landlords did not report tenancy as it could hamper their occupancy rights. The passing of the Goalpara Tenancy Act, 1922 increased the fear of the landlords in even the Ryotwari districts (Saikia 2014).

8. The big landholders included the la-khirajdars, nisf-khirajdars, zamindars in Goalpara and Karimgang, and the planters.

3

A Sketch of Assam's Agrarian Set-up

The primary focus of the present work is on the implications of tenancy for agricultural production. However, tenancy relations do not exist in isolation; rather, they prevail within a larger agrarian set-up. Hence, before narrowing the focus of the study to tenancy, an analysis of some aspects of the agrarian set-up of Assam based on available secondary data and other independent studies is presented here. The analysis presented sets the context for what will be discussed in the subsequent chapters.

An Overview of the Agriculture Sector in Assam

Role of Agriculture in the Economy of Assam

As per the statistics provided by the Economic Survey, Assam, 2014–15, while the major contributor to the Gross State Domestic Product (GSDP) of Assam in 2013–14 was the service sector (59.30 per cent of GSDP at 2004–05 prices), industry and agriculture contributed 22.8 per cent and 17.90 per cent, respectively, in the same year. Insofar as the contribution of agriculture to the GSDP is concerned, it has come down over the years. In 2004–05, agriculture contributed 21.4 per cent to the GSDP, which came down to 17.90 per cent in 2013–14. Although the share of the agriculture sector in GSDP has declined over time, it continues to provide employment to more than half (53 per cent) of the total workforce of Assam (Government of Assam, 2011–12).

The growth of agricultural GSDP had been erratic throughout the past decade. During 2005–06 and 2008–09, the growth of agricultural GSDP (including forestry and logging, fishing and mining and quarrying) had been abysmal. In 2009–10, the growth rate of agriculture was impressive (6.5 per cent); however, this fell to only 1.1 per cent in 2011–12. In recent years, the sector has recovered and once again registered an impressive growth of 4.3 per cent in 2013–14 (Economic Survey, Assam, 2014–15).

Nature of Agriculture in Assam

LAND USE PATTERN

Table 3.1. Land Use Pattern

Land Use	*Percentage of Total Geographical Area*
Net sown area	35.80
Land not available for cultivation	33.45
Area under forest cover	23.61
Fallow land	1.63
Land under still water and waterlogged	2.27
Social forestry	0.16
Other cultivable land	5.5

Source: Author's calculations, based on data from the Statistical Hand Book, Assam, 2014.

As per the land utilisation statistics for the year 2011–12, presented in the Statistical Hand Book, Assam, 2014, 35.80 per cent of the total geographical area is net sown area, and the percentage of area not available for cultivation is 33.45 per cent. On the other hand, 23.61 per cent is under forest cover, followed by 1.63 per cent of fallow land. Land under still water and waterlogged is 2.27 per cent, the area under social forestry is 0.16 per cent, and other cultivable area is 5.5 per cent.

Natural and Agro-Climatic Divisions of Assam and Farming Systems Therein

The total geographical area of Assam is divided into three natural divisions, viz., the Brahmaputra Valley, Barak Valley, and the Hills. The Brahmaputra Valley comprises about 72 per cent of the total geographical area of the state, accommodating around

85 per cent of the population. On the other hand, about 12 per cent of the population resides in the Barak valley, which accounts for only 9 per cent of the geographical area of the state. The hills, comprising of two districts, Karbi Anglong and Dima Hasao, has 19 per cent of the geographical area, accommodating only a little more than 3 per cent of the population.

While the state is constituted of the above three broad natural divisions, it has been divided into six Agro-Climatic Zones, as shown in Table 3.2, based on climate, rainfall and temperature, terrain, soil characteristics, and land-use pattern.

The first five Agro-Climatic Zones, that is, the plains comprising the Brahmaputra Valley and the Barak Valley, are largely similar in terms of the farming system, whereas the hills differ distinctly from the plains in terms of the system of cultivation. The method of cultivation in the plains of Assam is almost similar to the method that exists in most parts of India (Bezbaruah 1994). Paddy, especially the one grown during the rainy season of summer and

Table 3.2. Divisions of Assam in Terms of Agro-Climatic Zones

Agro-Climatic Zone	*Districts*	*Crops Grown*
Hills	Karbi Anglong and Dima Hasao	Maize, ginger, and sugarcane
Barak Valley	Cachar, Hailakandi, and Karimgang	Rice, sugarcane, and potato
Lower Brahamaputra Valley	Kamrup, Goalpara, Dhuburi, Nalbari, Baksa, Barpeta, Chirang, Bongaigaon, Kokrajhar	Rice, rape and mustard, jute, potato, wheat and pulse
Central Brahmaputra Valley	Nagaon and Moriagon	Rice, rape and mustard, jute, pulses
Upper Brahmaputra Valley	Tinsukia, Dibrugarh, Sibsagar, Jorhat, and Golaghat	Rice, rape and mustard, and sugarcane
North Bank Plain	Dhemaji, Lakhimpur, Sonitpur, Darrang, Udalguri	Rice, rape and mustard, and sugarcane

Source: Adapted from http://online.assam.gov.in/agricultureandrrigation accessed on 1/7/2012.

harvested in winter (winter paddy), is the principal crop grown in the plains. Besides this, jute is also grown during the same time. On the other hand, crops like rape and mustard, potato, vegetables, and sugarcane are grown during the winter season when rainfall is sparse. These crops are, however, not grown on a large scale.

In the hills, the traditional practice of shifting (jhum) cultivation is still the predominant mode of farming. The practice of shifting cultivation is believed to be one major reason for the lower agricultural productivity in the two hill districts of Assam. These hilly areas have tremendous potential to grow horticultural crops (Economic Survey, Assam, 2011–12). But the introduction of cash crops, horticultural crops, and settled agriculture on terrace lands continues to be a challenge due to certain problems like inadequate infrastructure, lack of access to the market, etc.

Cropping Pattern in Assam

Table 3.3 represents the cropping pattern in Assam. The cropping pattern is dominated mainly by food grains. Almost 80 per cent of the cropped area is under food grains. Again, within food grains, cereals, or more precisely rice, has the largest acreage share (72.51 per cent in 2013–14) in the gross cropped area (GCA).

Table 3.3. Cropping Patterns in Assam (% Share in Gross Cropped Area)

Sl. No.	*Crops*	*2011–12*	*2012–13*	*2013–14*
a	Total Rice	75.84	72.73	72.51
b	Total Cereals	76.85	74.62	74.28
c	Total Pulses	3.83	4.15	4.35
d	Total Food Grains (b+c)	79.67	78.71	78.62
e	Total Oilseeds	8.57	9.53	9.41
f	Total Fibres	2.09	2.08	2.17
g	Total Fruits and Vegetables	5.81	5.76	5.94
h	Miscellaneous Crops	3.86	3.92	3.82

Source: Author's own calculations, based on data taken from Statistical Handbook of Assam, 2014, Directorate of Economics and Statistics, Government of Assam.

Another important crop in terms of acreage share is oilseeds. While oilseeds account for a little more than 9 per cent of the GCA, 5.94 per cent of the GCA was devoted to fruits and vegetables in 2013–14.

Growth of Agricultural Production in Assam

Table 3.4 presents the compound annual growth rates (CAGR) of agricultural production between 2001–02 and 2010–11. The growth rates have been estimated for the production of food grains, non-food grains, and all crops separately. A semi-log trend equation has been fitted to the index numbers of the production of food grains, non-food grains, and all crops to calculate these growth rates.

Table 3.4. Estimated CAGR of Production of Food Grains, Non-Food Grains, and All Crops in Assam from 2001–02 to 2010–11

Crops	*CAGR (%)*
Food Grains	1.9
Non-food Grains	1.3
All Crops	1.6

Source: Author's own calculations, based on data taken from Economic Survey, Assam, 2011–12.

The CAGR for all crops between 2001–02 and 2010–11 was a modest 1.6 per cent. Again, while the production of food grains had grown at a rate of 1.9 per cent during the same period, that of non-food grains had grown at the rate of 1.3 per cent. This implies that the contribution of food grains to the growth of the overall agricultural production had been more relative to that of non-food grains during the last decade in Assam.

While food grains had contributed predominantly to the growth of agricultural production in the last decade, within food grains the contribution of rice to the total food grains production was the highest. Rice is the most important food crop not only in terms of production, but also in terms of the acreage share in the total cropped area, as is evident from Table 3.3.

Rice being the most prominent crop in Assam, an analysis of the growth performance in terms of area under production and yield of rice has been undertaken and presented in Table 3.5. The growth rates have been estimated by fitting a semi-log trend equation to area under production, total production and yield of rice between 2004–05 and 2013–14. During the period under consideration, the growth rate of rice production was an impressive 6 per cent. While the growth rate of the area was only 1 per cent during the same period, the growth rates of yield for autumn rice, winter rice, and summer rice were 6 per cent, 4 per cent and 6 per cent, respectively. In other words, the growth of rice production between 2004–05 and 2013–14 was made possible by the increase in the yield of rice.

Table 3.5. Estimated CAGR of Area, Production, and Yield of Rice in Assam from 2004–05 to 2013–14

Area		*1.00*
Production		6.00
Yield	Autumn Rice	6.00
	Winter Rice	4.00
	Summer Rice	6.00

Source: Author's own calculations, based on data from the Economic Survey, Assam, 2014–15.

THE AGRARIAN SET-UP IN ASSAM

Pattern of Landholding

As per the Agricultural Census 2005–06, there were 2,750,000 operational holdings in Assam, and the average size of an operational holding was only 1.11 hectare. Besides, the overwhelming majority of farmers were small and marginal farmers. The NSS data also reveals a similar picture.

Table 3.6 shows the distribution of ownership holdings and area owned, and Table 3.7 shows the operational holdings and area operated, respectively, by broad-size categories, as shown in various NSS reports.

Table 3.6. Percentage Distribution of Ownership Holdings and Area Owned in Assam by Broad-size Categories

Year	*Ownership Holdings*						*Owned Area*					
	L	*ME*	*SM*	*S*	*M*	*LL*	*L*	*ME*	*SM*	*S*	*M*	*LL*
1971–72	0.11	2.38	9.73	18.20	69.58	-	1.64	15.20	30.79	30.22	22.15	-
1981–82	0.09	1.87	9.34	22.00	66.69	-	1.48	11.50	27.67	34.81	24.53	-
1991–92	0.08	1.13	6.29	14.82	77.69	-	1.29	8.53	23.06	29.07	38.05	-
2002–03	0.00	0.50	3.60	14.20	81.80	-	0.00	4.32	16.36	34.87	44.42	-
2013	0.00	0.52	4.55	14.85	72.67	7.42	0.00	3.90	18.31	33.56	44.22	0.00

Notes: LL – Landless; M – Marginal; S – Small; SM – Semi-medium; ME – Medium; L – Large; '-' implies not available.

Source: Adapted from Table no. S4.2, NSS Reports No. 571, 70th Round, p. 56.

In terms of ownership holding, marginal holding had been the predominant category in all the time periods. The share of marginal holding in total ownership holding had increased from 69.58 per cent in 1971–72 to 81.80 per cent in 2002–03 (Table 3.6), which then fell to 72.67 per cent in 2013. However, this fall in the share of marginal holding in 2013 may be due to the inclusion of the additional category of 'landless' while classifying ownership holdings by size categories. Although previous NSS surveys provide information on the extent of landlessness, they did not take into account 'landless' as a separate category for the purpose of categorising the households by sizes of ownership holdings. In terms of area, while the share of marginal holding had increased from 22.15 per cent in 1971–72 to 44.42 per cent in 2002–03, those of all but small categories had come down over the same period. In 2013, however, the shares of marginal, small, and medium categories decreased slightly as compared to their respective shares in 2002–03, whereas the opposite was the case for the semi-medium category.

In summary, what can be observed from Table 3.6 is that the marginal, small, and semi-medium categories had been predominant throughout in terms of both ownership holdings and area owned. On the other hand, while the share of the medium category in ownership holdings and area owned had consistently fallen over time, that of the large category had been very negligible, and in fact has been nil since 2002–03.

Table 3.7. Percentage Distribution of Operational Holdings and Area Operated in Assam by Broad Size Categories

Year	*Operational Holdings*					*Area Operated*				
	L	*ME*	*SM*	*S*	*M*	*L*	*ME*	*SM*	*S*	*M*
1971–72	0.1	3.0	14.3	30.2	52.4	0.7	12.2	30.5	34.9	21.6
1981–82	0.1	2.7	11.3	24.3	61.6	1.4	13.7	29.3	33.5	22.1
1991–92	0.2	1.5	7.5	20.0	70.8	2.6	9.1	22.9	31.2	34.2
2002–03	0.0	0.6	4.7	18.4	76.2	0.00	4.9	17.1	36.0	42.0
2012–13	0.00	0.56	6.14	20.39	72.91	0.00	3.78	19.44	36.53	40.21

Note: M – Marginal; S – Small; SM – Semi-medium; ME – Medium; L – Large.
Source: Adapted from Table no S5.3, NSS Reports No. 571, 70th Round, p. 61.

As in the case of ownership holding, the overwhelming presence of the marginal and small categories, with an increasing share of the marginal category (barring in 2012–13), can also be discerned in terms of operational holding and area operated from Table 3.7. The share of marginal holding in total operational holding increased from 52.4 per cent in 1971–72 to 76.2 per cent in 2002–03, which then fell to 72.91 per cent in 2012–13. On the other hand, the share of operated area under marginal holding increased from 21.6 per cent to 42 per cent between 1971–72 and 2002–03, and fell to 40.21 per cent in 2012–13 (Table 3.7). While the shares of small and semi-medium categories in operational holdings and area operated in 2012–13 increased slightly as compared to 2002–03, the opposite is the case for the medium category. Like ownership holdings and area owned, marginal, small, and semi-medium categories had been the most dominant categories in all the periods, in terms of operational holdings and area operated.

Incidence of Tenancy in Assam's Agrarian Set-up

The National Sample Survey and Agricultural Census and Farm Management Studies of the Ministry of Agriculture are the two main sources of secondary data on landholdings and tenancy. Comparing these two sources, Sharma (1995) points out that the data on tenancy provided by the Agricultural Census are not fully reliable. Hence, before looking into the incidence of tenancy in Assam on the basis of the available secondary data, the limitations of these data have been briefly discussed.

Limitations of the Available Secondary Data

Although it sets out to collect data in terms of operational holdings, the Agricultural Census ends up collecting information in terms of ownership holdings only. This happens because of the source it relies upon. For records on landholdings, the Agricultural Census depends solely on revenue records. However, tenancy contracts are not entered into the revenue records due to two reasons: (*a*) most tenancy contracts are oral and informal, and (*b*) due to the restrictive tenancy laws, the owners of land do not usually reveal this information, even if they lease out their lands. Consequently, it appears that those who own land also operate it. Thus, the data on tenancy provided by the Agricultural Census is a gross underestimation of the magnitude and incidence of tenancy, and hence is completely unreliable. This shortcoming was exposed to this author by the personnel involved in conducting such Censuses themselves.

In the context of Assam, while the Agricultural Census of 1995–96 shows a miniscule incidence of tenancy, the 2000–01 Census exhibits a complete absence of it. According to the

Agricultural Census of 1995–96, the number of operational holdings wholly leased-in was only 0.023 per cent of the total operational holdings. Of the total number of operational holdings, 99.52 per cent was wholly owned and self-operated. In terms of area, while 99.01 per cent of the total operated area was self-operated, only 0.043 per cent was wholly leased-in. On the other hand, according to the Agricultural Census of 2000–01, the wholly leased-in area was nil; 99.97 per cent of the operated area was wholly owned and self-operated. Thus, the Agricultural Censuses give the impression that there is no incidence of tenancy in Assam.

In opposition to the findings of the Agricultural Censuses, independent studies show that a large part of the operated area is under lease or tenancy in Assam. For example, a study conducted by the Lal Bahadur Shastri National Academy of Administration in 1994 showed that more than half of the operated land in the surveyed area of Assam was wholly leased-in, with sharecropping being the predominant term of contract. The NSS data also suggest that like most parts of India, land is leased-in under various forms of tenancy contracts in Assam. However, it can be noted here that the incidence and magnitude of tenancy as represented by the NSS data is much less than those shown by various independent studies. The fact that the NSS also underestimates the incidence of tenancy has already been established by many studies (Ramachandran 1980; Ramakumar 2000; Sharma and Dreze 1998).

The NSS data, although not free from error, is comparatively comprehensive and based on the scientific methodology of data collection. However, it should be noted here that NSS data involves certain conceptual problems[1] that affect its temporal comparability. For example, operational holding has been defined differently in various rounds. The eighth round considered a much wider definition than presented in the 16th and 17th rounds.[2] The definition was even wider in the 37th round. Such problems are present in the case of tenancy data too. While the eighth round did not provide detailed information on the incidence of tenancy, the 16th and 17th rounds almost ignored the subject. Again, while the 26th round considered only three types of tenancy contracts to show the distribution of the leased-in land, the 37th round included another two forms of tenancy contracts in addition to those considered in the 26th round. Another limitation of NSS data in this context is that it does not explain anything about the nature of tenancy contracts included under the term 'other contracts', although these account for a sizable amount of the land leased-in in many states.

Different Dimensions of Tenancy in Assam, Based on NSS Data

INCIDENCE AND MAGNITUDE OF TENANCY IN ASSAM

Table 3.8. Percentage of Tenant Holdings and Leased-in Area in Total Operational Holdings and Operated Area

	Tenant Holdings in Total Operational Holdings				*Leased-in Area in Total Operated Area*			
	2012–13	*2002–03*	*1991–92*	*1981–82*	*2012–13*	*2002–03*	*1991–92*	*1981–82*
Assam	8.00	8.90	10.10	12.90	4.30	5.30	8.90	6.40
India	13.70	9.90	11.00	15.20	10.20	6.50	8.30	7.20

Source: Adapted from Statement S5.6, NSS report no. 571, 70th round.

The shares of tenant holdings in total operational holdings and leased-in area in total operated area, as shown in Table 3.8, have come down over different NSS surveys in Assam. While the share of tenant holdings came down from 12.9 per cent in 1981–82 to 8.00 per cent in 2013, the area leased-in fell from 6.4 per cent in 1981–82 to 4.30 per cent in 2013. On the other hand, for the country as a whole, shares of tenant holdings and area leased-in fell from 15.2 per cent and 7.2 per cent in 1981–82 to 9.9 per cent and 6.5 per cent in 2002–03, which then increased to 13.70 per cent and 10.20 per cent in 2013, respectively.

Table 3.9 shows the distribution of the tenant holdings and area leased-in in terms of the major forms of tenancy contracts. Sharecropping continues to be the prominent form of tenancy contract in terms of both holdings and area in Assam. As per the NSS survey, 2013, 55.80 per cent of the leased-in area was under sharecropping in Assam. The next important contract is fixed money. It can be mentioned here that a substantial amount of holdings and area come under 'other terms', which does not specify the nature of tenancy contracts. At the national level, however, fixed rent tenancy has emerged as the dominant tenancy contract as per the latest NSS survey (70th round, 2013) on household ownership and operational holdings in India. Thus, in 2013, fixed rent constituted 57 per cent (41.9 per cent under fixed money and 15.1 per cent under fixed produce) of the total leased-in area (NSS report no. 571, 2013), while only 28.4 per cent of the leased-in area was under sharecropping.

Table 3.9. Percentage Distribution of Tenant Holdings and Leased-in Area by Terms of Tenancy in Assam

Year	*Holdings*					*Area*				
	FM	*FP*	*SC*	*Service*	*OT*	*FM*	*FP*	*SC*	*Service*	*OT*
2002–03	–	–	–	–	–	15.80	3.60	55.00	–	25.60
2013	21.30	10.81	38.65	19.89	9.35	17.30	10.90	55.80	2.26	13.74

Note: FM – Fixed Money; FP – Fixed Produce; SC – Sharecropping; OT – Other Terms.
Source: Calculated from NSS reports no. 492 and 571, 59th and 70th rounds.

DURATION OF TENANCY CONTRACTS IN ASSAM

Table 6R of NSS report no. 492 (2002–03) shows that the duration of tenancy contracts for the major portion of the leased-in area was short. In Assam, in the kharif season, 22.09 per cent of the total leased-in area was cultivated by leasing-in for one agricultural season to less than one agricultural year. Of the total area, 25.79 per cent was leased-in for one agricultural year to less than two agricultural years, and 15.29 per cent was leased-in for two agricultural years to less than five agricultural years. A similar picture can be seen in the case of the rabi season as well. However, in the rabi season, the share of land leased-in for less than one agricultural season is slightly higher than that in the kharif season. The short duration of tenancy contracts has serious implications for long-term agricultural development and agricultural productivity. Tenants who lease-in land for short durations may not be interested in making investments for the improvement of land and to enhance productivity.

Distribution of the Lessees and Lessors by Social Groups in Different Size Classes of Ownership Holdings[3]

Tables 3.10 and 3.11 show the distribution of the households leasing-out and leasing-in, respectively, according to social groups.

Table 3.10. Percentage Distribution of Households Leasing-out Land and Average Area Leased-out for Each Social Group in Different Size Classes of Ownership Holding

	% of Households				*Average Area (in Hectare)*			
Ownership Holdings (in Hectare)	*ST*	*SC*	*OBC*	*Others*	*ST*	*SC*	*OBC*	*Others*
Nil	-	-	-	-	-	-	-	-
≤.002	-	-	-	-	-	-	-	-
0.002–0.005	-	-	-	-	-	-	-	-
0.005–0.04	-	-	-	-	-	-	-	-
0.04–0.50	-	82.80	71.2	48.00	-	0.266	0.266	0.199
0.50–1	-	-	0.65	0.47	-	-	0.399	0.067
1–2	57.40	16.50	17.6	23.80	1.194	1.018	0.762	0.796
2–3	28.20	-	0.42	12.30	1.451	-	1.311	0.622
3–4	0.620	-	0.02	0.17	3.345	-	0.533	1.743
4–5	0.29	-	-	0.96	1.862	-	-	1.739
5–7.50	0.54	-	-	-	4.014	-	-	-
7.50–10	-	0.06	0.03	-	-	4.776	3.331	-
10–20	-	-	-	-	-	-	-	-
≥20	-	-	-	-	-	-	-	-
All Size	100	100	100	100	1.571	0.419	0.416	0.561

Note: '-' implies not present in the size class.
Source: Calculated from Table 7, NSS report no. 571, 2013, p. A336.

The lessors are predominantly in the marginal and small categories of ownership holding for all social groups, especially for the SCs and the OBCs (Table 3.10). The average area leased-out for all size classes is the highest, that is, 1.571 hectares, among the ST group.

Table 3.11. Percentage Distribution of Households Leasing-in Land and Average Area Leased-in for Each Social Group in Different Size Classes of Ownership Holding

	% of Households				*Average Area (in Hectare)*			
Ownership Holdings (in Hectare)	*ST*	*SC*	*OBC*	*Others*	*ST*	*SC*	*OBC*	*Others*
Nil	0.42	64.40	64.50	32.00	0.282	0.362	0.080	0.007
≤.002	–	–	–	–	–	–	–	–
0.002–0.005	–	0.28	–	0.03	–	0.400	–	0.586
0.005–0.04	–	–	0.81	0.48	–	–	0.353	0.377
0.04–0.50	69.50	29.70	27.00	45.80	0.650	0.533	0.613	0.467
0.50–1	22.20	0.26	0.01	11.10	0.785	0.430	1.081	0.533
1–2	0.41	0.01	0.02	0.58	1.045	0.268	0.187	0.451
2–3	–	0.05	–	0.03	–	0.667	–	0.558
3–4	–	–	0.01	–	–	–	0.267	–
4–5	–	–	–	–	–	–	–	–
5–7.50	–	–	–	–	–	–	–	–
7.50–10	–	–	–	–	–	–	–	–
10–20	–	–	–	–	–	–	–	–
≥20	–	–	–	–	–	–	–	–
All Size	100	100	100	100	0.681	0.417	0.248	0.377

Note: '-' implies not present in the size class.

Source: Calculated from Table 8, NSS report no. 571, 2013, p. A414.

Table 3.11 shows that like the lessors, the lessees also mainly fall within the small and marginal category across all social groups. The average area leased-in by the STs is 0.681 hectare, followed by 0.417 hectare by the SCs and 0.248 hectare by the OBCs.

It can be observed from Tables 3.10 and 3.11 that while for the STs and the OBCs the average size of the land leased out is considerably higher than the average size of the land leased-in, the difference is negligible for the SCs.

Independent Studies vs. the NSS Data: The Case of Concealed Tenancy

According to the 70th round of NSS survey (2012–13), in the context of Assam, 8.00 per cent of the total operational holdings were tenant holdings and the percentage of leased-in area in the total operated area was only 4.30 per cent. However, this might be just an indication of the extent and magnitude of tenancy in the state; the actual magnitude may be much higher, as shown by many independent studies.

A study conducted in Assam in 1994 by the Land Reform Unit of the Lal Bahadur Shastri National Academy of Administration (LBSNAA), Mussoorie, revealed that concealed tenancy was widely prevalent in the state. Hence, referring to the figures in NSS reports and comparing them with the findings from the field survey, it concluded that NSS figures might have underestimated the magnitude of tenancy in the state. The LBSNAA study showed that 58.7 per cent of the total tenant holdings found during the field survey was unrecorded. These unrecorded tenants operated 73.3 per cent of the total operated area in the surveyed region. This is indicative of the prevalence of concealed tenancy and also of the underestimation of the magnitude of tenancy in the NSS surveys in the state. There are a few other studies which have also found that tenancy in Assam is extensive. In Lakhimpur district of Assam, Kuri (2003) found that while 8.7 per cent of the total operational holdings were pure tenant holdings, owner-cum-tenant holdings accounted for 47 per cent of the total. Bezbaruah (1994) found that 42 per cent of the sample farmers had land on lease as parts of their operational holdings.

Some Related Observations from Literature

So far as the term of contract is concerned, the NSS findings concur with the findings from independent studies. Sharecropping, according to both NSS surveys and other independent studies, is the dominant form of contract. While the 70th round of NSS survey estimated that 55.80 per cent of the total leased-in area was under sharecropping, the study conducted by the LBSNAA (1994) recorded that 78.3 per cent of the leased-in area was under this contract. This study further found a high incidence of informal sharecropping. The sharecroppers were invariably paying 50 per cent, or sometimes even more, as the share of the gross produce, in spite of sharing the input cost. Further, the study found that the two main reasons as to why the people leased-out were lack of capital resources and small size of holdings.

Bezbaruah (1994) found that tenancy takes a variety of forms, but sharecropping was the most frequently found form, with the practice of sharing of output between landlord and tenant at a 50:50 ratio. He also observed that tenancy was generally temporary and informal. Tenancy, of course, had not been found to have inhibited the adoption of new technology.

Kuri's study (2003) found that 95 per cent of the leased-in area was under sharecropping. He found that within sharecropping there were two variants of the contract, viz., *Guti adhi* and *Guchi adhi*. In the case of Guti adhi, grains are equally divided between the landlord and the tenant after the tenant harvests the crop. On the other hand, under Guchi adhi the ripe crop in the field is equally divided, and the landlord and tenant harvest their respective shares. He further found that owned land, the number of agricultural workers, and bullock endowment and human resources, as indicated by the level of education of the farmers, influenced the leasing decision of households in Assam. As for the human resource, it was found that with the increase in the level of education, the preference for non-farm employment increases, which in turn increases the tendency to lease out. He hence concluded that formal education leads to a higher incidence of tenancy, resulting in productive and allocative inefficiency in Assam's agriculture.

Gautam (1995) found that sharecropping was the most prominent type of tenancy for principal crops, whereas fixed rent was given 'over-riding prominence in respect of other crops'. The study further observed that tenancy relations prevailed only by way of verbal agreement. The available legislative measures were weakly implemented, only to germinate the feeling of insecurity of tenure among tenants, which had demoralised them and led them to not adopt any progressive farming practices.

Thus, in summary it may be said that although NSS data are qualitatively better relative to the Agricultural Census, the NSS also underestimates the extent and magnitude of tenancy. A comparison of NSS data on the incidence of tenancy with the findings from independent studies establishes this fact. This limitation of the data necessitates a primary survey of the households owning and operating agricultural land, so as to assess the real magnitude of tenancy. Besides, the data provided by the NSS are not sufficient to fathom the economic implications of the agrarian institution of tenancy comprehensively, for which additional data are required from the field.

NOTES

1. Sharma (1995) has discussed the problems of NSS data in detail.

2. The definition of operational holding in the eighth round included cultivable and non-cultivable land, land used for both agricultural and non-agricultural purposes, provided these holdings came under the management of a distinct technical and economic unit. However, in the 16th and 17th rounds, only the land used for agricultural purposes was considered as operational holding. But in the 37th round, the land used for rearing livestock, dairy, and pisiculture was also included under operational holding.

3. Lessees are those who lease-in land and lessors are the ones who lease-out.

4

THE CURRENT TENANCY SITUATION IN ASSAM[1]

As *discussed in Chapter* 3, the secondary data do not provide sufficient information on many dimensions of the tenancy relation. Hence, a primary survey was conducted in the plains of Assam. Taking the Assam plains as a case study and using the data generated there, this chapter and the next delve into the economic implications of the agrarian institution of tenancy.

A BRIEF DESCRIPTION OF THE SAMPLE

Composition of the Sample

The primary data for this work was collected during 2011–12 from the plains of Assam. Eighty-one per cent of the geographical area of Assam, comprising the Brahmaputra valley and the Barak valley, is plain and the rest (19 per cent) comprises of hills. The plains of the state differ characteristically from the hills in terms of agricultural system, institution, and climate. While shifting cultivation is still the predominant form of cultivation in the hills, settled cultivation is practised in the plains. The shift to individual title of land from community possession is not yet complete in the hills. However, people have individual ownership of land in the plains. In terms of climate, the major difference between the hills and the plains, or even within the plains, has to do with rainfall received. The hills receive a fairly low amount of rainfall, compared to the plains. While the Barak valley receives more rainfall compared to the Brahmaputra valley, the variations in the normal rainfall received in different zones within the Brahmaputra valley are not substantial. On the whole, however, the two valleys are considerably similar in terms of agrarian institutions and types of agricultural production. Hence, the collection of primary data was confined to only the plains of the state of Assam.

While collecting data, a multi-stage sampling process was adopted in order to make the sample representative of the target population from the plains of Assam. In the first stage, four non-contiguous districts were selected so as to capture the agro-climatic variations within the plains. The districts selected are Dibrugarh, Morigaon, Nalbari, and Cachar, which fall under the upper Brahmaputra valley, central Brahmaputra valley, lower Brahmaputra valley, and Barak valley, respectively. Since Barak valley constitutes only 9 per cent of the geographical area of the state and has only two districts, only one district was selected from this valley. In the second stage of sampling, one development block from each of these four districts was selected. These blocks were selected in such a manner so that they represented the prevailing cropping pattern and socio-economic characteristics of the districts. The district agriculture officers of the selected districts were consulted while selecting the blocks. The third stage of the

Figure 4.1. Procedure for Selecting the Sample

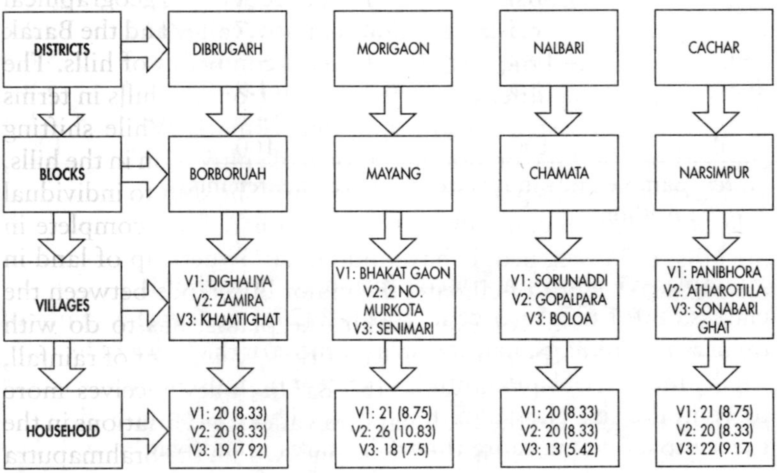

Source: Author.
Notes: V1 – Village 1; V2 – Village 2; V3 – Village 3.
Figures within ( ) represent percentages of households in the village in the sample.

sampling involved selecting three villages at random from each block. Finally, from each of the sample villages, 10 per cent of the households either owning or operating agricultural land were selected randomly. Thus, the final sample came to be comprised of 240 households. The selection process of the sample has been encapsulated in Figure 4.1.

Distribution of Sample Households in Terms of Ownership Holding and Operational Holding

Table 4.1. Percentage Distribution of the Sample Households under Different Size Classes of Ownership Holding

Ownership Holding (in Hectare)	*Field Study Locations*				*Overall*
	Dibrugarh	*Morigaon*	*Nalbari*	*Cachar*	
Nil*	11.9	15.4	18.9	14.3	15.0
0–1	30.5	40.0	37.7	41.3	37.5
1–2	30.5	23.1	35.8	22.2	27.5
2–3	8.5	9.2	5.7	12.7	9.2
3–4	10.2	3.1	–	6.3	5.0
4–5	8.5	6.2	1.9	3.2	5.0
5–6	–	3.1	–	–	0.8
Total	100	100	100	100	100

Note: *Sample units in this category are pure tenants.
Source: Author.

Table 4.1 shows a concentration of households in the size classes of 0–1 (37.5 per cent) and 1–2 (27.5 per cent) hectares of ownership holdings. In other words, most of the households own small amounts of land. Only 0.8 per cent of households are found to be in the size class of 5–6 hectares. There is no household in the sample owning more than 6 hectares of cultivable land. The disquieting finding, however, is that 15 per cent of households in the sample do not possess any agricultural land, or are landless. The percentage of landless households in Nalbari is even higher (18.9 per cent).

In terms of area, as shown in Table 4.2, while the largest share (32.44 per cent) is still that of the small class of 1–2 hectares of ownership holding, areas in the size classes of 3–4 (13. 72 per cent) and 4–5 (17.67 per cent) hectares are also not insignificant. Except for Nalbari, where more than 50 per cent of the sample area is in the size class of 1–2 hectares, the above general pattern also represents the patterns of ownership of agricultural land in the other three locations of field investigation.

Table 4.2. Percentage Distribution of Areas of Sample Farms under Different Size Classes of Ownership Holding

Ownership Holding (in Hectare)	*Field Study Locations*				*Overall*
	Dibrugarh	*Morigaon*	*Nalbari*	*Cachar*	
0–1	9.63	16.92	23.1	17.20	15.75
1–2	30.85	25.37	53.94	28.32	32.44
2–3	12.98	15.68	14.66	24.19	16.82
3–4	22.76	7.76	–	18.1	13.72
4–5	23.78	21.34	8.3	12.19	17.67
5–6	–	12.93	–	–	3.6
Total	100	100	100	100	100

Source: Author.

When the findings from Tables 4.1 and 4.2 are put together, it becomes evident that while 65 per cent of households (37.5 per cent + 27.5 per cent) in the size classes of 0–1 and 1–2 hectares own 48.19 per cent (15.75 per cent + 32.44 per cent) of the total area, only 10 per cent (5 per cent in each) of sample households in the size classes of 3–4 and 4–5 hectares own 31.39 per cent (13.72 per cent + 17.67 per cent) of the sample area. These findings testify to the existence of inequality in landholding.

In terms of operational holding, both in the case of the number of operational holdings (Table 4.3) and area of sample farms (Table 4.4), most of the sample households are in the size classes of 0–1, 1–2, and 2–3 hectares. In other words, on the whole most

Table 4.3. Percentage Distribution of the Sample Households under Different Size Classes of Operational[2] Holding

Operational Holding (in Hectare)	*Field Study Locations*				*Overall*
	Dibrugarh	*Morigaon*	*Nalbari*	*Cachar*	
Nil*	8.5	7.7	7.5	7.9	7.9
0–1	22.0	43.1	32.1	41.3	35.0
1–2	37.3	29.2	39.6	36.5	35.4
2–3	20.3	10.8	15.1	14.3	15.0
3–4	5.1	6.2	1.9	–	3.3
4–5	5.1	1.5	3.8	–	2.5
5–6	1.7	1.5	–	–	0.8
Total	100	100	100	100	100
Average Size (in hectares)	*1.70*	*1.26*	*1.34*	*1.09*	*1.34*

Note: *Sample units in this category are pure lessors.
Source: Author.

Table 4.4. Percentage Distribution of Areas of the Sample Farms under Different Size Classes of Operational Holding

Operational Holding (in Hectare)	*Field Study Locations*				*Overall*
	Dibrugarh	*Morigaon*	*Nalbari*	*Cachar*	
0–1	9.21	19.31	16.12	24.59	16.59
1–2	30.91	31.89	40.90	44.59	36.27
2–3	30.24	19.36	26.58	30.82	26.78
3–4	10.55	16.91	4.71	–	8.64
4–5	14.02	6.02	11.69	–	8.48
5–6	5.07	6.51	–	–	3.24
Total	100	100	100	100	100

Source: Author.

farms are small and marginal farms, and a similar pattern can be observed across field study locations. In Cachar, especially, all the farms are small and marginal, although a few households operating some amount of area in the subsequent higher size classes can be found in the other three locations. There is no farm in the present sample operating on over 6 hectares of land. The average size of operational holding for the entire sample is found to be 1.34 hectares. In Dibrugarh, the average size of operational holding is, however, a little higher (1.70 hectares) than the overall average.

Table 4.5. Distribution of Sample Households across Size Classes of Ownership Holdings for Size Classes of Operational Holdings (in %)

Operational Holding (in Hectare)	*Ownership Holding (in Hectare)*						
	NIL	0–1	1–2	2–3	3–4	4–5	5–6
Nil	–	*3.3*	*13.6*	*9.1*	*16.7*	*16.7*	*50*
0–1	61.1	**54.4**	*12.1*	*9.1*	*16.7*	*8.3*	–
1–2	27.8	34.4	**56.1**	*22.7*	*8.3*	*8.3*	–
2–3	5.6	6.7	15.2	**59.1**	*16.7*	*25*	–
3–4	2.8	1.1	1.5	–	**41.7**	–	–
4–5	2.8	–	1.5	–	–	**33.3**	–
5–6	–	–	–	–	–	8.3	**50**
Total	100	100	100	100	100	100	100

Source: Author.

Distribution of the sample households across size classes of ownership holding over size classes of operational holdings has been shown in Table 4.5. Here, the rows and columns show the available size classes of operational holdings and ownership holdings, respectively. The first column under ownership holding, that is, NIL, represents the landless pure tenant households who operate entirely on leased-in land; they are essentially small farmers. The figures falling on the diagonal (in bold, for example the third column under ownership holding and third row under operational holding) denote the farmers who operate and own equal amounts of land. For instance, in the size category of 1–2 hectare, 56.1 per cent of the households are on the diagonal who, in that size class, are the owner-operators. The figures to the right of the diagonal (in italics) are the households who either do not operate on any land or operate on land less than the owned land. As, for instance, 12.1 per cent of households in the size category of 1–2 hectares of ownership holding operate on only 0–1 hectare, implying a leasing-out of land by these households.[3] Thus, the households above the diagonal are the lessors. The opposite is the case with households to the left of the diagonal. These households are the lessees, for whom the size of operational holdings is higher than that of the ownership holdings. If each size class is analysed in this manner, the following two findings emerge: (*i*) owner-operators are the prominent category in all size classes; and (*ii*) the proportions of lessors increase with the size of the ownership holding. Although there may still be some lessee households in the higher size class of ownership holding, the proportion of lessors is substantially higher relative to lessees. For example, in the size class of 4–5 hectares of ownership holding, only 8.3 per cent of the households are lessees in comparison to 58.1 per cent of lessors, and the remaining 33.3 per cent owner-operators. This suggests an absence of reverse tenancy in the state.[4]

MAGNITUDE AND PATTERNS OF TENANCY AND DURATION OF TENANCY CONTRACTS

Magnitude of Tenancy: Number of Tenant Households and Areas of Sample Farms under Lease

In terms of tenure status, the sample households can be distributed over five different categories, as shown in Table 4.6. The pure tenants are those who do not own any cultivable land and hence lease-in land from others to operate. In contrast are the pure lessor households who, while owning agricultural land, do not operate on any land; rather, they lease out the entire land.

Owner-operators cultivate the agricultural land that they own. On the other hand, besides operating on their own land, the owner operator-cum-tenant households lease-in additional land, whereas the owner operator-cum-lessor households operate on a part of their own land and lease out the rest. In the present

Table 4.6. Sample Households by Tenure Status (in %)

Field Study Locations	*Pure Tenant*	*Owner-Operator*	*Owner Operator-cum-Tenant*	*Owner Operator-cum-Lessor*	*Pure Lessor*	*Total*
Dibrugarh	11.86	33.90	40.68	5.09	8.47	100
Morigaon	13.8	32.3	36.92	9.2	7.7	100
Nalbari	18.9	34	34	5.7	7.5	100
Cachar	14.3	23.8	27	25.4	9.5	100
Overall	15	30.8	34.2	11.7	7.9	100

Source: Author.

sample, the highest number of households (34.2 per cent) belongs to the owner operator-cum-tenant category. The next largest category is owner-operator, followed by pure tenant and owner operator-cum-lessor, and the smallest category is that of the pure lessor. While 30.80 per cent of the total sample households are owner-operators, 15 per cent, 11.7 per cent, and 7.9 per cent of the total sample households are pure tenant, owner operator-cum-lessor, and pure lessor, respectively. Thus, Table 4.6 shows that 49.2 per cent of the sample households (pure tenant and owner operator-cum-tenant taken together) have either fully or partially leased-in land, or are tenants.

Table 4.7 shows that about one-third of the overall (32.84 per cent) sample area is under lease and the remaining (67.16 per cent) area is owner-operated.

Table 4.7. Proportion of the Sample Operational Holding under Lease

Field Study Locations	*Leased-in Area*	*Owned*	*Total*
Dibrugarh	28.5	71.5	100
Morigaon	31.15	68.85	100
Nalbari	41.75	58.25	100
Cachar	32	68	100
Overall	32.84	67.16	100

Source: Author.

Thus, while about 50 per cent of the sample farmers are tenants (fully or partially), almost one-third of the operated area in the sample is leased-in area (Tables 4.6 and 4.7). All the tenancy contracts prevailing in the field study locations happen to be informal or oral, indicating that concealed tenancy is widespread in Assam.

Location-wise Patterns of Tenancy Contracts

Table 4.8. Tenant Farmers by Terms of Lease (as a Percentage of Total Sample Tenant Farmers)

Field	*Fixed Rent*			*Sharecropping*			
Study Locations	*In Cash*	*In Kind*	***Total***	*With Cost Sharing*	*Without Cost Sharing*	***Total***	*Mortgage*
Dibrugarh	25.00	5.56	**30.56**	5.56	47.21	**52.77**	16.67
Morigaon	7.32	65.85	**73.17**	9.76	4.88	**14.64**	12.19
Nalbari	11.43	22.86	**34.29**	5.71	48.57	**54.28**	11.43
Cachar	–	3.70	**3.70**	85.18	7.42	**92.60**	3.70
Overall	11.51	27.34	**38.85**	22.30	27.34	**49.64**	11.51

Source: Author.

Table 4.9. Area under Lease by Terms of Lease (as a Percentage of Total Leased-in Area)

Field	*Fixed Rent*			*Sharecropping*			
Study Locations	*In Cash*	*In Kind*	***Total***	*With Cost Sharing*	*Without Cost Sharing*	***Total***	*Mortgage*
Dibrugarh	33.26	7.49	**40.75**	7.03	43.33	**50.36**	8.90
Morigaon	19.32	63.19	**82.51**	8.36	2.35	**10.71**	6.79
Nalbari	5.19	18.51	**23.70**	9.03	53.27	**62.30**	**14.00**
Cachar	–	4.57	**4.57**	88.11	5.49	**93.60**	1.83
Overall	15.12	23.47	**38.59**	24.73	28.34	**53.07**	8.35

Source: Author.

The two main tenancy contracts found in the field study locations are fixed rent and sharecropping. Although insignificant, mortgage is another type of tenancy arrangement.[5] Further, there are variants of fixed rent and sharecropping. For example, a fixed rent contract may be in the form of a fixed money or fixed produce contract. On the other hand, sharing of the costs of cultivation between the tenant and the lessor may be combined with sharing of output in certain cases under sharecropping. In such cases, the lessors usually supply the seed retained from his/her previous year's share of produce. Only in a few cases have the lessors paid the expenses for fertilisers and tilling the land, over and above providing the seed.

Tables 4.8 and 4.9 further reveal that between fixed rent and sharecropping, the latter form of tenancy contract is the largest one. Half of the tenant farmers (49.64 per cent) are sharecroppers, with a little more than half the leased-in area (53.07 per cent) being under this contract. On the other hand, 38.85 per cent of the tenants are fixed rent tenants who operate on 38.59 per cent of the total leased-in area. Although on the whole sharecropping and fixed rent are the major types of tenancy contracts, the choice of tenancy contracts across field study locations is not uniform. While 92.60 per cent of tenant farmers leased-in land under sharecropping in Cachar, 73.17 per cent of tenant farmers are fixed rent tenants in Morigaon. The area under sharecropping in Cachar and that under fixed rent in Morigaon are 93.60 per cent and 82.51 per cent of the total area under lease in these two locations, respectively. In Dibrugarh and Nalbari, too, sharecropping seems to be the relatively preferred tenancy arrangement, with more than half the tenant farmers leasing-in land under this contract. It can be further observed from Tables 5.8 and 5.9 that within fixed rent and sharecropping, the mode of contract varies across location. For example, while in Dibrugarh rent is paid in cash under most fixed rent tenancy arrangements, rent in kind is the predominant mode of fixed rent contract in Morigaon. On the other hand, although sharing of the costs of cultivation is the usual arrangement under sharecropping in Cachar, the same is not the case in Dibrugarh and Nalbari.

Table 4.10. Lessors by Terms of Lease (as a Percentage of Total Lessors)

Field Study Locations	*Fixed Rent*			*Sharecropping*			*Mortgage*
	In Cash	*In Kind*	**Total**	*With Cost Sharing*	*Without Cost Sharing*	**Total**	
Dibrugarh	–	–	–	25.0	75.0	100	–
Morigaon	6.25	50.0	56.25	37.5	–	37.5	6.25
Nalbari	–	–	–	28.57	71.43	100	–
Cachar	–	–	–	91.30	4.35	95.65	4.35
Overall	1.85	14.82	16.67	57.41	22.22	79.63	3.70

Source: Author.

Table 4.11. Areas Leased out by Terms of Lease (as a Percentage of Total Leased-out Area)

Field Study Locations	*Fixed Rent*			*Sharecropping*			*Mortgage*
	In Cash	*In Kind*	**Total**	*With Cost Sharing*	*Without Cost Sharing*	**Total**	
Dibrugarh	–	–	–	32.14	67.86	100	–
Morigaon	17.92	46.24	64.16	34.41	–	34.41	1.43
Nalbari	–	–	–	33.01	66.99	100	–
Cachar	–	–	–	97.39	1.04	98.43	1.57
Overall	3.72	19.21	22.93	42.81	33.21	76.02	1.05

Source: Author.

While Tables 4.8 and 4.9 show the location-wise preferences towards forms of tenancy contracts when land is leased-in, Tables 4.10 and 4.11 show the same in the case of land being leased out. These two tables confirm the findings of Tables 4.8 and 4.9, the exception being that there is no lessor leasing-out land under fixed rent in Dibrugarh, Nalbari, and Cachar. This only establishes the predominance of sharecropping more strongly in general, and particularly in these three locations.

Why does the pattern of tenancy contracts vary across locations? Why is it that most tenant farmers prefer a fixed rent tenancy arrangement in Morigaon, while in the remaining three locations the tenants are mostly sharecroppers? Answers to these questions may be derived from the cropping patterns prevailing in specific locations. The prevailing cropping patterns across the field study locations and tenure statuses have been shown in Tables 4.12 and 4.13, respectively. An analysis of these two tables reveals that selection of a tenancy contract by a tenant depends on the crop that is grown by him/her.

Table 4.12. Cropping Pattern across Field Study Locations

Field Study Locations	*Winter Paddy*	*Summer Paddy*	*Potato*	*Winter Vegetable*	*Rape and Mustard*	*Jute*
Dibrugarh	74.38	–	2.79	24.58	0.5	–
Morigaon	18.65	53.53	–	5.43	23.72	–
Nalbari	78.67	11.79	1.21	4.08	2.98	3.91
Cachar	75.09	18.74	3.75	2.42	–	–
Overall	58.18	22.09	1.74	9.37	7.78	0.84

Source: Author.

Table 4.13. Cropping Pattern across Tenure Statuses

Tenure Status	*Winter Paddy*	*Summer Paddy*	*Potato*	*Winter Vegetable*	*Rape and Mustard*	*Jute*
Owner Operator	58.35	21.67	2.21	9.15	7.72	0.90
Sharecropping	88.37	9.4	0.48	–	1.31	0.44
Fixed rent	22.12	39.36	0.39	21.54	16.2	0.39
Overall	58.18	22.09	1.74	9.37	7.78	0.84

Source: Author.

Table 4.12 demonstrates that as a whole, the most prominent crop is winter paddy, with 58.18 per cent of the total cropped area under this crop. The second largest share of the cropped area is devoted to summer paddy (22.09 per cent), which is followed by winter vegetable (9.37 per cent) and rape and mustard (7.78 per cent).

However, it emerges from an inquiry into the cropping patterns existing in specific field study locations that while around 75 per cent of the cropped area is under winter paddy in Dibrugarh, Nalbari, and Cachar, summer paddy (53.53 per cent), followed by rape and mustard (23.72 per cent), are the major crops cultivated in Morigaon. On the other hand, it also appears that sharecropping exists predominantly in the locations where winter paddy is the most important crop, in terms of the operated area devoted to this crop. By contrast, fixed rent prevails largely in Morigaon where summer paddy has the largest cropped area under it. Thus, what transpires from the above discussion is that when tenants choose to grow winter paddy, they like to lease-in land under sharecropping. The reason for preferring sharecropping when winter paddy is cultivated is that the crop grown during the rainy season is exposed to more weather-related risk and uncertainty, as compared to crops grown during other seasons. Sharecropping allows the tenants to share the risk related to the crop, along with the output. Hence, tenants like to lease-in land under sharecropping when they choose to cultivate a crop like winter paddy.

This, however, is not the case with crops such as summer paddy, winter vegetables, and rape and mustard. These crops are subject to little weather-related risk, which encourages the application of expensive inputs for production, such as high-yielding variety seeds, chemical fertilisers, pesticides, irrigation, and so on, while cultivating these crops. Application of these better quality inputs minimises production risk and increases the production and productivity of, as well as returns from, these crops, which further induces farmers to grow these crops largely on a commercial basis. Thus, owing to the absence of weather-related risk, minimisation of production risk, and increased production, productivity, and returns, the tenants prefer fixed rent contracts for growing these crops, which allows them to retain the entire returns. This explains why Morigaon, where the principal crops grown are summer paddy and rape and mustard, has an overwhelming presence of fixed rent tenancy. Further, when the crop grown is winter vegetable, rent in cash is the preferred mode of contract, since vegetables are perishable. This explains the significant presence of fixed rent in cash in Dibrugarh, where a sizeable proportion of the sample cropped area is devoted to growing winter vegetables (24.58 per cent).

Table 4.13 endorses the above discussion. It shows that winter paddy is grown on 88.37 per cent of the total operated area under sharecropping. By contrast, a total of 77.10 per cent of the area under fixed rent is devoted to summer paddy, winter vegetables, and rape and mustard.

Across field study locations, there are substantial variations in the rent charged, especially rent in cash, under fixed rent contracts (Table 4.14). While the maximum cash rent is Rs 3,000 and the minimum is Rs 200, the average cash rent prevailing in three locations is calculated to be Rs 1,220 per bigha of land. As far as rent in kind is concerned, the average, maximum, and minimum rents paid against per bigha of leased-in land are 3.19, 5, and 2 mounds of paddy, respectively. The average rent in both cash and kind is found to be the highest in Morigaon, in comparison to other locations.

In order to understand the variations in rent within and across locations, rent per hectare (in thousand rupees) has been regressed on certain variables which can potentially affect variations in rent. These variables are: inequality in landownership, access to employment in the non-farm sector, operational holding under HYV seeds as a proportion of the total operational holding, irrigated operational holding as a proportion of the total operational holding, expenditure on capital goods on each hectare of operational holding, access to credit and two locational dummies.[6] The details of the regression analysis have been presented in Appendix 4A. The regression analysis reveals that no variables, except for access to credit and two locational dummies, have significant influence on variations in rent per hectare. Access to credit impacts the rent paid positively since having access to credit allows the tenants to use greater doses of expensive inputs like HYV seeds; the tenants may therefore be able to pay more rents from the resulting higher returns. It is interesting to note that inequality of landholding and technology used in cultivation (captured by area under HYVs, irrigation and capital expenditures) have no impacts on the rent paid, which warrants an explanation.

Tables 4.1 and 4.2 reveal that notwithstanding some amount of inequality in landholding, most sample households are, however, marginal, small and, at best, semi-medium landholders. This implies that the incidence of inequality in landholding may not be too high to have a significant impact on rent paid while leasing-in land. The fact that marginal and small categories include the overwhelming proportion of ownership holdings holds not only for the field study locations, but also for the entire state, which is evident from various rounds of the National Sample Survey reports (see Table 3.6). As far as technology is concerned, it may not impact rent significantly since technology is chosen by the tenant after finalising the lease contract. Hence, technology does not enter into the negotiation of rent. In fact, for irrigation also, it is a matter of a tenant's choice rather than of its availability, as shallow tubewells are the primary source of irrigation for the tenants in the sample.

On the other hand, the coefficients of two locational dummies have been found to have significant impacts on variations in rent across locations. The size of the coefficients of the locational dummies imply that the rent on an average is higher in Nalbari and Morigaon by Rs 280 and Rs 580, respectively, as compared to Dibrugarh. This finding is indicative of the fact that the explanation for variations in rent across locations has to be sought in differences in the residual locational characteristics, like fertility and pressure of population on agricultural land. One would expect the rent to be higher in locations where pressure on land and the fertility of land are higher. Taking the number of the rural population against per hectare of net area sown as an indicator of the pressure of population on agricultural land, one finds that among the three locations under consideration, pressure on agricultural land is maximum in Nalbari, followed by Morigaon and Dibrugarh.[7] On the other hand, fertility of land is the highest in Dibrugarh, a bit less in Morigaon, and much lower in Nalbari, as reflected in the trend of the yield rate of rice (Figure 4A.1).[8] Thus, Morigaon happens to be the location where fertility and pressure of population on agricultural land are neither low nor very high; rather, it falls somewhat in between those in Dibrugarh and Nalbari. Hence, both factors come into force, resulting in relatively higher rents in Morigaon. In Dibrugarh, however, although fertility of agricultural land is higher, the pressure of population on land is lower. The opposite is the case in Nalbari. To put it differently, one factor may counterbalance the other in Dibrugarh and Nalbari, which is the probable reason for the prevalence of almost equal average rents in these two places. The marginally higher average rent in Nalbari, as compared to that in Dibrugarh, may be the result of a relatively higher demand for land under lease in the former location (see Table 4.7).

As far as sharecropping is concerned, the tenants retain only half the produce while the remaining half goes to the lessors, even in those cases where the lessors do not share any part of the costs of

Table 4.14. Tenancy Contracts and Corresponding Rental Arrangements

Types of Tenancy Contracts		*Dibrugarh*	*Morigaon*	*Nalbari*	*Cachar*	*Overall*
Fixed rent in cash (in Rs/per bigha)	Average	811	2,000	850	-	1,220
	Maximum	1,000	3,000	1,500	-	3,000
	Minimum	500	1,000	200	-	200
Fixed rent in kind (in mound/ per bigha)	Average	3	3.85	2.9	3	3.19
	Maximum	4	5	3	3	5
	Minimum	2	3	2.5	3	2
Sharecropping with cost sharing (share of output)		50–50	50–50	50–50	50–50	50–50
Sharecropping without cost sharing (share of output)		50–50	50–50	50–50	50–50	50–50
Variants of sharecropping		*Guchi aadhi and Muthi aadhi*	*Guti aadhi*	*Guti aadhi*	*Guti aadhi*	*Guchi, Guti and Muthi*

Note: One maund = 40 kg, and one bigha = 0.13387 hectares.
Source: Author.

cultivation. This arrangement is prevalent in all the locations. Since land is leased-in under sharecropping to grow winter paddy and the crop is grown under the same state of affairs in all locations, rent in terms of share of produce does not vary. However, the portion of produce that goes to the lessors exceeds the amount specified in the existing tenancy legislation of the state by a substantial margin. The lessor may demand a higher share, considering a part of the produce as insurance premium, as they also bear a part of the weather and production risk associated with winter paddy.[9] Although output is shared in the same proportion across locations, three variants of the sharecropping contract—*Guti Adhi, Guchi Adhi*, and *Muthi Adhi*—could be found in the field study locations. While Muthi Adhi and Guchi Adhi exist in Dibrugarh, the variant of sharecropping that prevails in the remaining locations is the Guti Adhi. In the case of Guchi Adhi, the paddy field is divided into two equal parts, and the lessor and tenant harvest their respective parts. Muthi Adhi refers to the arrangement where the tenant, after harvesting the crop, hands over his/her share to the lessor, and the tenant and lessor then process their respective shares. In the case of Guti Adhi, the tenant harvests and processes the crop and then provides one half of the *guti* (that is, the seeds) to the lessor.

Duration of Tenancy Contracts

It has been found that more than 60 per cent of the tenancy contracts are for less than three years. This is applicable for both sharecropping and fixed rent tenancy contracts (Tables 4.15 and 4.16). The reason for the short duration of the majority of tenancy contracts may be a stringent provision in the prevailing tenancy laws in the state. As per this provision, a tenant may first turn into an occupancy tenant and then finally into the owner of the leased-in land if s/he grows crops on the land for three successive years.[10] Owing to this provision, most lessors do not want to lease out land for more than three years continuously, even if the contracts are not formally recorded.

The short length of the tenancy contracts may have an adverse consequence insofar as the sustainable use of agricultural land is concerned. Short durations may reduce the incentive of the tenants to undertake any measures to develop the land. Moreover, the tenants may not be mindful while applying inputs like chemical fertilisers, since their objective will be only to earn as much returns from the land as possible during the specified short period of contract. Excessive application of such inputs may adversely impact the natural fertility of land. The fixed rent tenant may be particularly tempted to do so, given the incentive structure within which they operate.

Table 4.15. Tenancy Contracts under Fixed Rent by Duration of Lease (in %)

Field Study Locations	*Duration of Lease*						
	One agri. Season	*1–2 Years*	*3–6 Years*	*7–9 Years*	*10–14 Years*	*15–20 Years*	*Total*
Dibrugarh	–	45.5	45.5	9.1	–	–	100
Morigaon	25	45	20	10	–	–	100
Nalbari	13.6	54.5	18.2	–	4.5	9.1	100
Cachar	–	100	–	–	–	–	100
Overall	14.8	50	24.1	5.6	1.9	3.7	100

Source: Author.

Table 4.16. Tenancy Contracts under Sharecropping by Duration of Lease (in %)

Field Study Locations	*Duration of Lease*							
	<3 Years	*3–6 Years*	*7–9 Years*	*10–14 Years*	*15–19 Years*	*20–24 Years*	*25-30 Years*	*Total*
Dibrugarh	71.4	28.6	–	–	–	–	–	100
Morigaon	66.7	33.3	–	–	–	–	–	100
Nalbari	47.4	36.8	5.3	–	5.3	–	5.3	100
Cachar	60	24	8	–	–	4	4	100
Overall	60.8	29.7	4.1	–	1.4	1.4	2.7	100

Source: Author.

SOCIO-ECONOMIC CHARACTERISTICS OF LESSEES AND LESSORS

We have already discussed that most of the owners of land and farmers fall in the marginal, small, or at best, medium categories (see Tables 4.1 and 4.3). In fact, in the sample, not a single household operates on or is in possession of land greater than 6 hectares. Thus, it is obvious that the tenants and lessors would also be mainly from the above three categories of operational and ownership holdings.

Distribution of Lessees and Lessors in terms of Social Groups, Education and Primary Occupation of Family

Figure 4.2. Lessees and Lessors by Social Groups (in %)

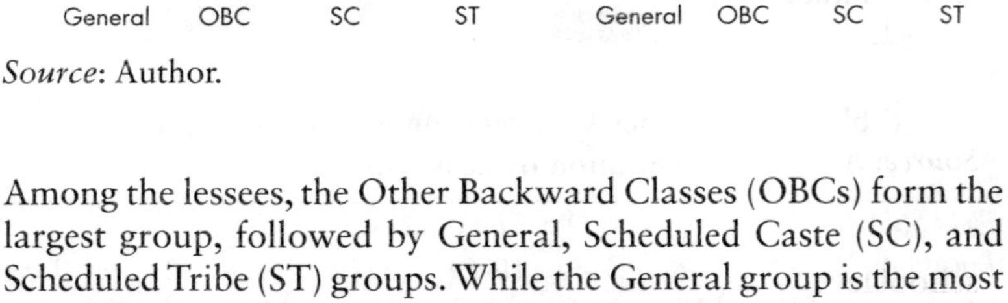

Source: Author.

Among the lessees, the Other Backward Classes (OBCs) form the largest group, followed by General, Scheduled Caste (SC), and Scheduled Tribe (ST) groups. While the General group is the most prominent among the lessors, the OBC is the next largest group. Only 18.81 per cent of the lessees are SC and ST, taken together. On the other hand, while only 6.25 per cent of the lessors are SC, there is no lessor from the ST group (Figure 4.2).

As presented in Figure 4.3, the education level of the majority of lessees is low. The proportion of lessees who are not literate is 27 per cent. While 14 per cent of the lessees have education of below primary level, another 46 per cent have primary to high-

Figure 4.3. Lessees and Lessors by Level of Education (in %)

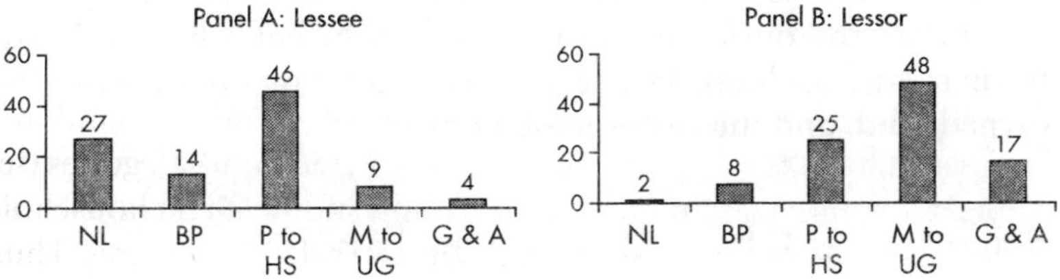

Note: NL – Not Literate; BP – Below Primary; P to HS – Primary to High School; M to UG – Matriculate to Undergraduate; G &A – Graduates and Above.
Source: Author.

Figure 4.4. Primary Occupation of the Families of Lessees and Lessors (in %)

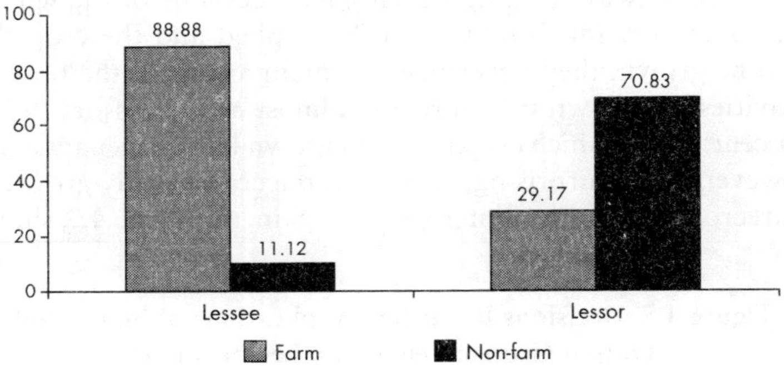

Source: Author.

school level of education. Only a few of the lessees are matriculates and graduates. By contrast, most of the lessors have acquired a relatively upper level of education. While the proportion of not literate among the lessors is negligible (2 per cent), 65 per cent of them are matriculate or above.

As is evident from Figure 4.4, lessees are primarily employed in the farm sector. The proportion of lessees who depend on the farm sector for livelihood is as high as 88.88 per cent. On the other hand, only 29.17 per cent of the lessors depend primarily on the farm sector and the remaining 70.83 per cent have their primary employment in the non-farm sector. Those 29.17 per cent of the lessors are the ones who do not have sufficient labour relative to their landholdings. Hence, they operate only on a portion of owned land, and the rest is leased out.

Some Further Observations on the Lessors

Lessors and Sharecropping

It appears from Figure 4.5 that taking a decision regarding the application of inputs and crops to be grown is largely a prerogative of the tenants. In 64.18 per cent of the cases, it is the tenant who takes these decisions, while the lessor alone has a say only in 13.43 per cent of the cases. Although the lessors stay away from influencing the decisions of the tenants regarding how much input is to be applied and the crop that is to be grown, they nevertheless remain aware of the tenants' activities. As shown in Figure 4.6, almost all the lessors (97.92 per cent) know which crop has been grown by their tenants; this, however, is not surprising, given that the crop usually grown on sharecropped land is winter paddy. Again, as Figure 4.7 shows,

Figure 4.5. Decisions Regarding Applications of Inputs and Output Grown: Tenant Vs. Lessor (in %)

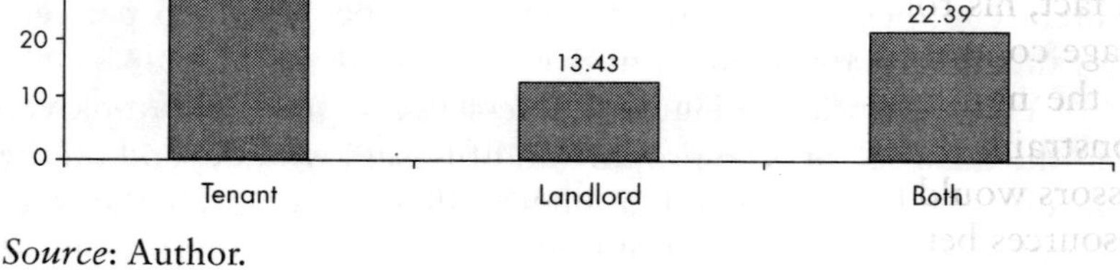

Source: Author.

90.7 per cent of the lessors monitor the application of inputs by the tenants. The question, however, that one might ask at this point is: Why do lessors choose to monitor this, especially when monitoring involves costs? The answer to this question is as follows. We have already mentioned that land is usually leased-in under sharecropping to grow winter paddy. As winter paddy is exposed to weather risk, it becomes easier for a tenant[11] to shirk his responsibility by attributing a bad harvest to bad weather. In other words, there is a possibility that lessors may face the problem of hidden action (information problem),[12] resulting in the principal-agent problem. The presence of the principal-agent problem may compel the lessors to monitor.

In the context of our sample, monitoring was feasible too. The lessors could monitor easily at a relatively lower cost as the majority (more than 80 per cent) of the plots of land leased out was within the same villages of their residence. This also points to the fact that there is little evidence of absentee landlordism. The absence of absentee landlordism and hence, the feasibility of monitoring, further suggests that the lessors could largely overcome the information problem. At this juncture, one may raise the question: Why do lessors not choose a wage contract even when they are not absentee lessors? Why do they settle for sharecropping, even when they could largely overcome the information problem? This is probably because the role that the lessor has to play when he chooses a sharecropping contract is completely different from the role he would otherwise play if the contract is a wage labour contract. Under sharecropping, the lessor's job is confined only to the occasional monitoring of the tenant's activities. On the other hand, the lessor's responsibility is two-fold under wage contract. Besides monitoring the work of the hired worker, the lessor will have to play the role of an organiser or manager. He will have to manage the entire farm; in fact, his role as manager assumes major significance under a wage contract. However, as most lessors are primarily engaged in the non-farm sector, they would face a critical managerial constraint if they choose a wage contract. In other words, the lessors would find it difficult to allocate their limited managerial resources between farm and non-farm activities simultaneously.

Figure 4.6. Percentage of Lessors who have Knowledge of Crops Grown by the Tenants

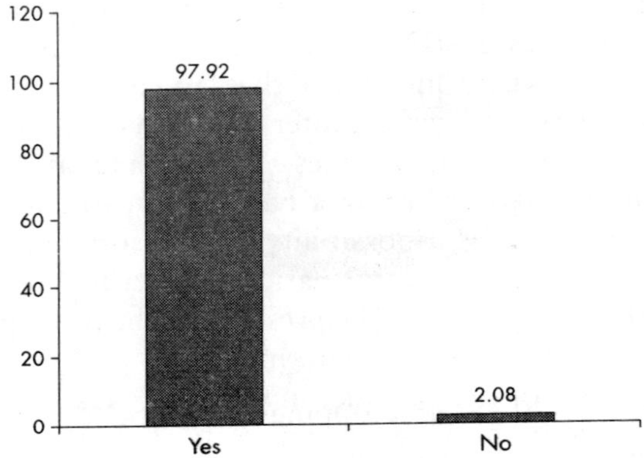

Source: Author.

Figure 4.7. Percentage of Lessors who Monitor the Application of Inputs

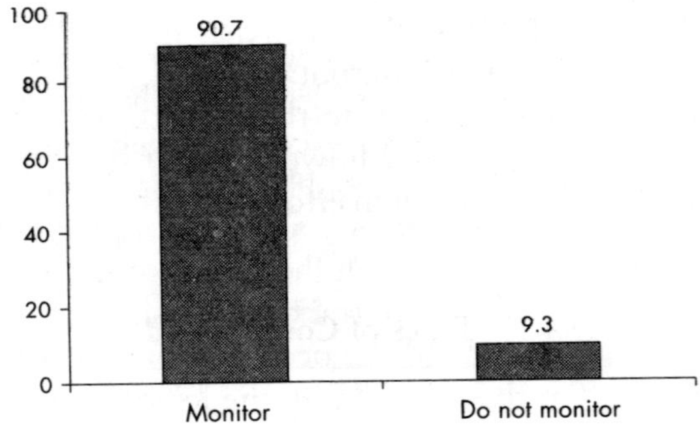

Source: Author.

A sharecropping or fixed rent contract would, however, allow the lessor to release his managerial resources from the farm sector and devote them to the non-farm sector. In fact, a lessor in the present context should ideally prefer fixed rent to sharecropping as that would release the entire managerial resource from the farm sector. However, a risk-averse tenant will not accept a fixed

Figure 4.8. Percentage of Lessors who have Shared Costs of Cultivation with the Tenants

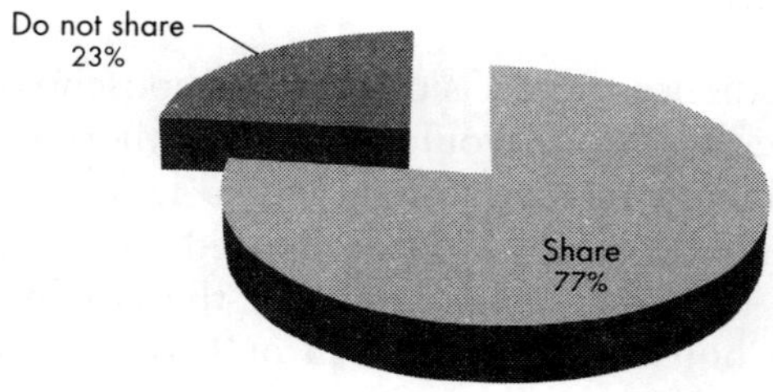

Source: Author.

rent contract. Thus, the sharecropping contract appears to be a compromise solution for the lessors.

Although the lessors do not devote much of their managerial resources to agricultural operation, many of them bear a part of the costs of cultivation. It has been found that 77 per cent (Figure 4.8) of the lessors share some part of the costs of cultivation with their tenants. However, in most cases (63.64 per cent) the lessors provide only the seeds (Table 4.17), which they have retained from their share of the previous year's output. In another 15.15 per cent of the cases, besides proving seeds to the tenants, they share the cost of fertilisers. Sharing of costs, however small an amount it is, may also induce the lessors to put in effort in terms of monitoring.

Table 4.17. Types of Costs Shared

Types of costs	*Percentage*
All	6.06
Tilling	6.06
Seed	63.64
Fertiliser and Seed	15.15
Fertiliser and Harvesting	3.03
Fertiliser and Pesticides	3.03
Fertiliser and Tilling	3.03
Total	100

Source: Author.

FACTORS INFLUENCING THE LEASING DECISION OF FARM HOUSEHOLDS

What influences the leasing decision of rural households? In the light of economic theory, one would expect that those households that have more labour relative to land would lease-in land from households that have more land compared to labour. Thus, endowments of land and labour may be the two influencing factors inducing households to lease-in or lease-out land. Kuri (2003) found that households with a relatively higher level of education tend to lease-out land. It is evident from the sample households as well that lessors are more educated as compared to the lessees. Thus, education may also be an important determinant of the leasing decision. Another impression that one gets from the sample is that access to non-farm employment may be a factor that impacts the leasing decision of households. It has been found that while 88.88 per cent of the lessees find employment primarily in the farm sector, 70.83 per cent of the lessors work mainly in the non-farm sector. Some other determinants of the leasing choice of households may be: the age of the household's head; irrigated land as a proportion of the total operational holding; access to credit; ownership of bullocks and ownership of machinery for tilling (Laha and Kuri 2011). To answer the question as to what influences a household's leasing decision, a regression analysis has been carried out in which the leasing decision has been regressed upon all these explanatory variables. Moreover, three locational dummies have been incorporated in the regression model so that the probable influence of agro-climatic differences across the field study locations on the sample households' leasing decision can be captured.

Construction of the Variables

Leasing decision (Y, that is, the dependent variable): The leasing decision of the households can be captured in terms of the magnitude of tenancy, that is, the total size of the leased-in or leased-out land by the households. However, such a measure of the magnitude of tenancy suffers from the limitation of being unable to reveal the correct intensity of the tenancy arrangement. For example, a big landowner may lease out a small proportion of her/his owned land and by absolute measure, s/he may look like a lessor even though the farmer is basically an owner-operator. Therefore, to get the correct picture, the amount of leased-in/out land has to be expressed in comparison to the total operational holding and/or the total ownership of land. However, one confronts a problem if only owned land or operational holding is used as the standardising element. The value that emerges when the absolute magnitude of tenancy is divided by only owned land is infinity as far as the pure tenants are concerned. A similar result arises for pure lessors when the absolute size of tenancy is divided by operational holding. Hence, in the present work, the summation of operational holding and owned land has been taken as the standardising factor.

Thus, Y = {(operational holding – land owned) / (operational holding + land owned)}

It transpires that Y will lie within the range of -1 to 1. If Y = -1, it is a pure lessor, Y= 0 when the farmer is an owner-operator, and Y= 1 for a pure tenant.

Farm worker (FW): The number of adults in a household who are mainly engaged in agriculture. Households with more farm workers are likely to lease-in more land. Thus, it is expected that the variable will influence the dependent variable positively.

Education (EDU): This represents the level of education of the head of the household. We hypothesise that education creates an aversion towards agriculture, and hence, the higher the level of education, the lower the amount of land leased-in. Thus, the coefficient of the variable EDU should bear a negative sign.

Occupation (FOCCUP): This is the dummy for the primary occupation[13] of a household. The variable takes the value 1 if the household is primarily engaged in the non-farm sector; otherwise, it takes the value 0 if farm occupation is the principal occupation of the household. It may be expected that a household in which the majority of members have non-farm employment would lease out land to release labour and other household resources for their better utilisation in the non-farm sector. Thus, *a priori*, the coefficient of the variable is expected to have a negative sign.

Age (AGE): This is the age of the head of the household in years. The expected sign of the coefficient of the variable is negative, as an older farmer may not be able to lease-in more land.

Ownership of Bullock (OB): This is a dummy variable with D = 1 if the household owns bullocks, and 0 otherwise. Households in possession of a bullock are expected to lease-in land, and hence the expected sign of the coefficient is positive.

Ownership of Tilling Equipment (OTE): This is a dummy variable with D = 1 if the household owns tractor/power tiller, and 0 otherwise. Households in possession of tractor/power tiller are expected to lease-in land, and hence the expected sign of the coefficient is positive.

Access to Credit (ACR): This is a dummy variable with D = 1 if the household has access to bank credit, and 0 otherwise. Access to credit will allow a household to hire tilling machinery and purchase other inputs, which may induce the household to lease-in more land. Thus, the expected impact of the variable on leasing decision is positive.

Proportion of Area under Irrigation (PAIRR): This variable represents the area under irrigation as a proportion of the total operational holding. A household would like to lease-in more of such land where irrigation is available, and hence, the expected sign of the coefficient of the variable is positive.

Inequality in landholding (ILH): This is captured by the coefficient of variation of ownership holding at the village level, and the expected sign of the coefficient is negative as, *cetiris paribus*, an egalitarian landholding pattern would minimise the requirement of leasing-in or out.

Location Dummies: Taking Dibrugarh as the reference category, three dummies have been used, viz., L_1, L_2 and L_3, where L_1 = 1 for Morigaon, 0 otherwise; L_2 = 1 for Nalbari, 0 otherwise; and L_3 = 1 for Cachar, 0 otherwise.

Functional Specification of the Model

A linear regression model is considered inappropriate in the present context since the dependent variable takes values between

-1 and 1. The linear regression model is not appropriate as the predicted values from such a model may not always lie between the range of -1 and 1. Moreover, clusters of observations at both ends of the dependent variable, where it takes the values of -1 and 1, respectively, could be observed in the data set. Hence, a both side censored Tobit model is considered suitable in this context.

The Tobit model is formulated with the help of latent variable Y_i^* which may take any possible value but cannot always be observed. The final model estimated is formulated as in equation 4.1.

$$Y_i^* = \beta_0 + \beta_1 FW_i + \beta_2 EDU_i + \beta_3 FOCCUP_i + \beta_4 AGE_i + \beta_5 OB_i + \beta_6 OTM_i + \beta_7 ACR_i + \beta_8 PLHIRRI_i + \beta_9 ILH_i + \lambda_1 L_{1i} + \lambda_2 L_{2i} + \lambda_3 L_{3i} + U_i \text{ --------------- } (4.1),$$

where U_i is the random disturbance term.

The observed dependent variable Y_i is linked to the latent variable Y_i^* as per the following configuration:

$$\begin{aligned} Y_i &= -1 \text{ for } Y_i^* < -1 \\ &= Y_i^* \text{ for } -1 \leq Y_i^* \leq 1 \\ &= 1 \text{ for } Y_i^* > 1 \end{aligned}$$

STATA 10.0 has been used to obtain the Maximum Likelihood estimates of the parameters and the results are presented in Table 4.18.

Table 4.18. Results of the Both Side Censored Tobit Regression

Breusch-Pagan test for heteroskedasticity *Chi^2 [11] = 18.62** *Prob. = 0.0981* *Result: Presence of heteroskedasticity*	
Variables/Constant	*Estimates of the Coefficients*
FW	0.064**
	(0.029)
EDU	–0.161***
	(0.035)

(contd.)

(Table 4.18 contd.)

Breusch-Pagan test for heteroskedasticity *Chi^2 [11] = 18.62** *Prob. = 0.0981* *Result: Presence of heteroskedasticity*	
Variables/Constant	*Estimates of the Coefficients*
FOCCUP	–0.473***
	(0.090)
AGE	–0.007**
	(0.003)
OB	0.168
	(0.131)
OTE	–0.130
	(0.147)
ACR	0.065
	(0.101)
PAIRR	0.0001
	(0.0008)
ILH	–0.0054
	(0.2524)
L_1	–0.080
	(0.141)
L_2	0.114
	(0.129)
L_3	0.029
	(0.128)
Constant	0.753**
	(0.366)
Pseudo R^2	0.1973
F[12,228]	8.05***

Notes: Figures within ( ) and [ ] are robust standard errors and the degrees of freedom, respectively.
***,**,* indicate significant at 1, 5, and 10 per cent, respectively.
Source: Author.

Since the sample comprises of a cross-section of households, the Breusch-Pagan test has been applied to check if the problem of heteroskedasticity is present in the data set, and the result is found to be positive. Consequently, heteroskedasticity consistent robust standard error has been calculated to take care of the problem.

The results presented in Table 4.18 reveal that four of the explanatory variables have a significant impact on the leasing decisions of rural households. All the coefficients of the variables have the expected signs. The coefficient of FW has a positive sign and is significant at 5 per cent, which implies that the higher the number of farm workers in a household, the higher is the amount of land leased-in by that household. On the other hand, the coefficients of FOCCUP and EDU are negative and significant at 1 per cent. With respect to EDU, the result proves the hypothesis of the study to be correct, that is, with the increase in the level of education, people tend to withdraw from agriculture and prefer to lease out land. The negative and significant coefficient of FOCCUP implies that households primarily employed in the non-farm sector lease out land so as to facilitate better use of labour and other resources of the households in the non-farm sector. Finally, the variable AGE appears to have a negative and significant coefficient, implying that if the head of the household is relatively older, the amount of land leased-in by the household will be less.

SUMMARY OF THE FINDINGS

The agrarian institution of tenancy is widespread in the Assam plains, which is evident from the fact that almost half of the sample farmers are either fully or partially tenant farmers and around one-third of the sample farm area is under lease. All the people (lessors and lessees) involved in tenancy arrangements are marginal and small, or at best medium farmers, and there is little evidence of reverse tenancy. All the tenancy arrangements have been found to be informal contracts, implying that concealed tenancy is rampant in the state. Moreover, the majority of tenancy contracts are for short duration, which may have an adverse implication for the sustainable use of land.

Notwithstanding location-specific variations, sharecropping and fixed rent are found to be the major forms of tenancy contract prevailing in Assam. On the whole, between fixed rent and sharecropping, sharecropping is predominant in terms of the number of holdings and area under this contract. The explanation for the location-specific variations in the prevailing forms of tenancy contracts may be found in the cropping pattern prevailing in the field study locations.

Sharecropping exists largely in those locations where the main crop cultivated is winter paddy. Winter paddy involves weather risk, and as sharecropping is a contract which allows the tenants to share the risk related to the crop with the lessors, they prefer to lease-in land under sharecropping if they cultivate winter paddy. On the other hand, in spite of the lessors being able to overcome the information problem to a large extent, they still prefer sharecropping to wage contract as it allows them to release their managerial resources from the farm sector and devote them to the non-farm sector. Thus, it can be concluded that sharecropping contracts are more often the manifestations of attempts to manage risk by the tenant farmers, than the information problem of the landlords.

The findings from the regression analysis suggest that the number of farm workers in a household, the level of education of the head of the household, the primary occupation of the household, and the age of the head of the household are the factors that influence the leasing decision of the household. While households with more labour tend to lease-in land, with higher levels of education, people tend to lease out their farm land. The analysis also shows that households which are primarily employed in the non-farm sector lease out, as this allows the better use of the households' endowments of labour and other resources in the non-farm sector. Given these findings, one would expect that with an increase in the level of education and expansion of non-farm employment opportunities, more agricultural land will be available for lease. Hence, the challenge for policymakers will be to ensure efficient, equitable, and sustainable utilisation of these lands.

NOTES

1. A substantial part of this chapter has been published in the *Economic and Political Weekly* as 'Incidence, Forms and Determinants of Tenancy in the Agrarian Set-Up of the Assam Plains', XLVIII (42), 2013, 60–68.

2. Operational Holding = land owned + land leased-in – land leased-out – fallow land.

3. The possibility of keeping land fallow does not arise as the fallow land has been deducted from the owned land while calculating operational holding.

4. Reverse tenancy arises when small landholders lease out land to big farmers.

5. Under mortgage, the lessee pays an amount in cash to the lessor at the beginning of the contract. The amount to be paid is negotiated by the lessee and the lessor. The lessee continues to possess the land till s/he gets the money back from the lessor.

6. Prospective yields may arguably be a factor influencing rent. However, yield from land hinges partly on the characteristics of land, such as soil fertility and presence of irrigation, and to some extent on the inputs and practices used by the tenant. Some of the independent variables used in the regression model should take care of both sets of determinants of rent. Hence, yield as an independent variable affecting the rent agreed upon by the tenants and the lessors has not been incorporated separately in the regression analysis.

7. Rural population against each hectare of net area sown in Nalbari is 10.15, followed by 9.61 in Morigaon and 7.77 in Dibrugarh, respectively. These numbers have been calculated from data taken from the Economic Survey of Assam, 2011–12 and Handbook of Statistics, 2010 (Directorate of Economics and Statistics, Government of Assam).

8. Data on yield of crops in districts of Assam going back to before the advent of the Green Revolution (when technology did not have a role to play and yield was a function of natural soil fertility only) show that the yield of rice, especially winter rice (which in those years constituted 80–90 per cent of the gross cropped area), tended to be lower as one goes southwestwards from districts on the northeastern edge of the Brahmaputra valley (Phookan, et al. 1980). Data for recent years, presented in Figure 4A.1, confirm the persistence of this pattern. This evidence is indicative of the fact that the natural soil fertility tends

to decline continuously as one goes from the upper Brahmaputra valley to the central and lower Brahmaputra valley in Assam, that is, from Dibrugarh to Morigaon, and then to Nalbari.

9. However, when the costs of cultivation are shared, the landlord's share may not be excessive.

10. An occupancy tenant, after holding land for three successive years, gets heritable right of occupancy and use on the land.

11. An owner operator-cum-tenant may put in more effort on his land than on the leased-in land.

12. The information problem that results in the principal agent problem is of two types: (*i*) the problem of asymmetric information between the tenant (or hired labour) and the landlord regarding the former's skill; and (*ii*) the hidden action or moral hazard problem. The information problem is usually likely to accompany a wage contract, especially when the lessor (the principal) is an absentee lessor. Hence, under such circumstances, the lessor usually prefers a sharecropping contract. However, as our evidence suggests, the problem of hidden action may appear even under sharecropping. When the crop grown involves weather risk, a tenant (the possibility is greater in the case of an owner operator-cum-tenant) may shirk his responsibility and attribute a bad harvest to bad weather. However, the problem, whether under wage contract or sharecropping, can be overcome to a large extent if the lessor can monitor, or if he is not an absentee lessor.

13. If the majority of household members are mainly engaged in non-farm (farm) employment, then that household's primary occupation is non-farm (farm).

Appendix 4A

The regression model developed to identify the factors contributing to variations in rent under fixed rent contract within or across locations has the following exponential specification. The exponential formulation is preferred to linear specification on the ground that the dependent variable, that is, rent per hectare (in thousand rupees), takes only positive value.

$$Y_i = \exp(\beta_0 + \beta_1\,POHIRRI_i + \beta_2\,POHHYV_i + \beta_3\,CE_i + \beta_4\,CR_i + \beta_5\,ANFE_i + \beta_6 ILH_i + \beta_7 L_{1i} + \beta_8 L_{2i} + U_i) \quad \text{.............. (4A.i)}$$

Where, Y_i = rent per hectare of operational holding

POHIRRI = area under irrigation as a proportion of total operational holding

POHHYV = area under HYV seeds as a proportion of total operational holding

CE = expenditure on capital equipment per hectare of operational holding

CR= credit

ANFE = access to non-farm employment measured in terms of percentage of family members engaged in non-farm employment

ILH = inequality of landholding captured in terms of coefficient of variation of ownership holding at the village level

L_1 and L_2 are two locational dummies, where L_1 = 1 for Morigaon, 0 otherwise; L_2 = 1 for Nalbari, 0 otherwise. Dibrugarh is the reference category.

The above non-linear formulation of the regression model has been made linear by taking logarithm in both sides for ease of estimation. Thus, the final model estimated is the following:

$$\text{Ln}\,Y_i = \beta_0 + \beta_1\,POHIRRI_i + \beta_2\,POHHYV_i + \beta_3\,CE_i + \beta_4\,CR_i + \beta_5\,ANFE_i + \beta_6 ILH_i + \beta_7 L_{1i} + \beta_8 L_{2i} + U_i \quad \text{............ (4A.ii)}$$

Results of the regression analysis are presented in Table 4A.1.

Table 4A.1. Regression Results Explaining Locational Variations in Rent under Fixed Rent Contract

Breusch-Pagan test for heteroskedasticity
Chi^2 [7] = 9.57
Prob. = 0.2963
Result: No heteroskedasticity

Variables/Constant	*Estimates of the Coefficients*
POHIRRI	–0.0005
	(0.0013)
POHHYV	–0.0005
	(0.0012)
CE	–0.00001
	(0.000016)
CR	1.88*
	(1.14)
ANFE	0.0030
	(0.0025)
ILH	–0.025
	(0.243)
L_1	0.58***
	(0.13)
L_2	0.28**
	(0.12)
Constant	4.66***
	(0.256)
R^2	0.6304
F[8, 40]	8.53***

Notes: Figures within ( ) and [ ] are standard errors and the degrees of freedom, respectively.
***,**, * indicate significant at 1, 5, and 10 per cent, respectively.
Source: Author.

Figure 4A.1. Yield Rate of Rice in Some Field Study Locations

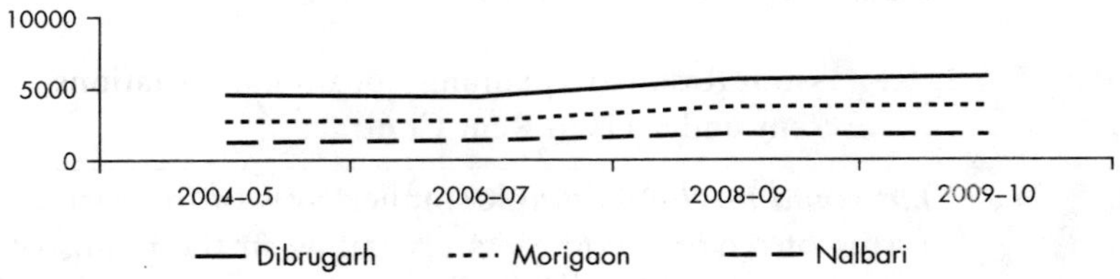

Source: Author.

5

IMPLICATIONS OF TENANCY ARRANGEMENTS

What could be the economic implications of the various forms of tenancy contracts prevailing in the plains of Assam, as documented in Chapter 4? Do they provide sufficient incentive to tenants to supply adequate efforts in crop production? Do various tenancy contracts induce tenants to adopt production and productivity enhancing practices differently? What is the implication of tenancy contracts for the sustainable use of agricultural lands? This chapter attempts to answer these questions.

To answer these questions, the following indicators of production and productivity enhancing practices have been considered: (*i*) cropping intensity, (*ii*) crop diversification, (*iii*) adoption of HYV rice, (*iv*) per hectare NPK (fertiliser) consumption, and (*v*) income generated within the farm. As for input intensities, labour and capital intensities have been taken into account. In order to isolate the effect of tenancy on production and productivity enhancing practices and on the input intensities, the following two methods have been espoused.

a) The first method involves a comparison of the above practices and input intensities of the owner operator-cum-tenant on his own land and leased-in land (sharecropped land and land under fixed rent are considered separately). This method, however, provides only some preliminary impressions and does not give any conclusive idea about the impacts of tenancy on production and productivity enhancing practices and input intensities. Nevertheless, the important objective that it satisfies is to take care of the problem of imperfection in rural markets and its implications for the efficiency of different tenure forms (Bell 1977).
b) The second method involves the isolation of the effect of tenancy in general, and various forms of tenancy in particular, on production and productivity enhancing practices and input intensities through the regression technique.

DEFINITION OF PRODUCTION AND PRODUCTIVITY ENHANCING PRACTICES AND INPUT INTENSITIES

Cropping Intensity (CI): This reflects how many times a farmer cultivates his land during one agricultural year. Cropping intensity = (Gross Cropped Area/Net Sown Area)*100. Cropping intensity is 100 if the land has been cropped only once in a year.

Crop Diversification (CD): In the present context, this has been defined in terms of the allocation of cultivable area by the farmers to facilitate a diverse crop portfolio. The Herfindahl Index has been used as a measure of the extent of crop diversification, which is constructed by using the following formula:

$$H = \sum_{i=1}^{N} s_i^2$$

where s_i is the share of the i-th crop in the total cropped area. The value of the index lies between 0 and 1. A movement within the range from 0 to 1 implies a more concentrated cropping pattern. For convenience of interpretation, we have, however, used (1-H) as the measure of crop diversification, in which the value of the index still lies within the range of 0 to 1, but with the opposite interpretation. Now a movement from 0 to 1 would reflect a greater extent of diversification.

Extent of Adoption of High-yielding Varieties Rice (HYVR): The area under HYV rice as a percentage of the total rice acreage has been considered an indicator of the extent of the adoption of HYVs.

Fertiliser Consumption (FC): NPK (in kg) per hectare of gross cropped area is considered to be the indicator of fertiliser consumption.

Gross Income Generated (IG)[1]: Value of the total farm output – total costs of purchased intermediate inputs used in all crops, where purchased intermediate inputs include fertilisers, pesticides, fuel, and irrigation charge. Again, the value of the total farm output is the summation of the market values of the crops produced.[2] Finally, the total income generated within the farm household during one agricultural year has been divided by the total operational holding of the household to obtain the income generated per hectare of operational holding by that household.

Labour Intensity (LI): The amount of labour used per hectare of gross cropped area has been used as the measure of labour intensity. The amount of labour has been expressed in value (monetary) terms, which is given by the product of the number of man days—both hired and family—and the existing wage rate.

Capital Intensity (CAPI): The definition of capital in the present context is confined only to the working capital. In other words, capital has been used as a flow concept rather than a stock. Thus, expenditures on capital include payment made in terms of rents of tractor, power tiller, pump-set and motor, and bullock pair. Expenditures incurred on the above items by a farm household constitute the total capital expenditures of that household. Finally, the total capital expenditure of a household is divided by the gross cropped area of the household to obtain the capital expenditure per hectare of gross cropped area, or capital intensity. In case a household owns capital equipment, the imputed value of the service of the equipment has been considered.

INDEPENDENT AND CONTROL VARIABLES USED IN THE REGRESSION ANALYSIS

Independent Variable

Tenancy is the variable of prime concern in the study and is used as the independent variable in the regression analysis for all indicators of production and productivity enhancing practices and input intensities. There are, however, five variants of the tenancy variable. The construction of five different forms of the tenancy variable is motivated by the necessity of examining the impact of tenancy in general, and that of its various forms in particular, separately. Accordingly, the following five alternate forms of the tenancy variable have been formulated:

i) Total Leased-in Area as a percentage of Operational Holding (LI).
ii) Leased-in Area under Sharecropping as a percentage of Operational Holding (SC).
iii) Leased-in Area under Fixed Rent as a percentage of Operational Holding (FR).
iv) Leased-in Area under Sharecropping without Cost Sharing as a percentage of Operational Holding (SCWCS).
v) Leased-in Area under Fixed Rent and Sharecropping with Cost Sharing together as a percentage of Operational Holding (FRSCCS).

While the first variant of the tenancy variable represents the total magnitude of tenancy or tenancy in general, the second and third variants have been constructed to disentangle the effects of sharecropping and fixed rent. The remaining two forms (the fourth and the fifth) further allow us to examine the impacts of another two types of tenancy contracts within sharecropping, that is, sharecropping with cost sharing and without cost sharing. The motivation for this further categorisation of sharecropping comes from the existing theoretical knowledge. The existing literature suggests that when the tenant and the lessor share the cost of cultivation, the tenant equates his marginal cost to the marginal product,[3] and hence the Marshallian inefficiency may be eliminated. Thus, a sharecropping contract with cost sharing arrangement is as efficient as a fixed rent contract. Hence, areas under fixed rent and sharecropping with cost sharing have been clubbed together to form the fifth variant, while keeping the area under sharecropping without cost sharing under the fourth variant of the tenancy variable.

Since the debate with respect to the relative efficiency/ inefficiency of various tenancy contracts is not conclusive, the significance and signs of the alternate specifications of the tenancy variable will determine whether tenancy and its various forms have a positive or negative effect on production and productivity enhancing practices and input intensities.

Control Variables Used in Different Regression Models[4]

CROPPING INTENSITY

Farm Size (FS): Size of operational holding in hectares has been used as a measure of the farm size.

Extent of Irrigation (IR): The extent of irrigation has been measured as the proportion of irrigated area in the operational holding.

Access to Extension (EXT): This is a dummy variable, where D = 1 if the i-th farmer has received any direct benefits from the government's extension service network; D = 0, otherwise.

While interviewing the farmers, six questions relating to the extension service were asked. Farmers' responses to these questions indicate whether they have received any direct benefits from the extension service. On the basis of the farmers' responses, the variable D has been assigned the value 0 or 1.

Access to Finance (FIN): This is a dummy variable, where D = 1 if the i-th farmer has access to institutional credit; otherwise, D= 0.

Area under High-Yielding Varieties (PHYV): This has been captured in terms of the percentage of area under HYV rice as a percentage of the total rice acreage.

Availability of Farm Labour (FL): The number of farm workers per hectare of operational holding in a household.

Location Characteristics: The locations of the field study fall in four different agro-climatic zones. Agricultural practices may vary across these agro-climatic zones, and hence the cropping intensity as well. Thus, taking Dibrugarh as the reference category, three dummies have been used, viz., L_1, L_2, and L_3; where L_1 = 1 for Morigaon, 0 otherwise; L_2 = 1 for Nalbari, 0 otherwise; and L_3 = 1 for Cachar, 0 otherwise.

CROP DIVERSIFICATION

The control variables used in the regression model for crop diversification are *Farm Size (FS)*, *Extent of Irrigation (IR)*, *Access to Extension (EXT), Access to Finance (FIN), Availability of Farm Labour (FL),* and *Locational Characteristics.* The definitions of the variables are the same as in the case of cropping intensity.

EXTENT OF ADOPTION OF HIGH-YIELDING VARIETIES RICE

The control variables used in the regression anaylsis for the extent of use of HYV rice are *Farm Size (FS), Extent of Irrigation (IR), Access to Extension (EXT), Access to Finance (FIN),* and *Locational Characteristics.* The definitions of the variables are as before.

FERTILISER CONSUMPTION

The control variables used in the regression model for fertiliser consumption are as follows: *Farm Size (FS), Extent of Irrigation (IR), Access to Extension (EXT), Access to Finance (FIN), Area under Fertiliser Intensive Crops (AFIC),* and *Locational Characteristics. Area under Fertiliser Intensive Crops (AFIC)* has been defined as the area under fertiliser-intensive crops as a percentage of the operational holding. The remaining control variables have the same definitions as before.

GROSS INCOME GENERATED

The following are the control variables used for the regression model of the gross income generated: *Farm Size (FS), Extent of Irrigation (IR), Access to Finance (FIN),* and *Locational Characteristics.* The definitions of the variables are as before.

LABOUR INTENSITY

The control variables used in the regression model for labour intensity are: *Family labour (FL), Area under Winter Paddy (AWP),* and *Locational characteristics.* The imputed value of family labour per hectare of gross cropped area has been taken as a measure of *family labour.* On the other hand, area under winter paddy as a proportion of the total cropped area has been used as a measure of the variable *AWP.*

CAPITAL INTENSITY

Farm Size (FS) and *Locational characteristics* have been used as control variables in the regression for capital intensity.

The expected signs of the coefficients or the potential direction of the impacts of the control variables on the indicators of production and productivity enhancing practices and input intensities have been summarised in Table 5.1.

Table 5.1. Expected Signs of Coefficients of Control Variables used in Different Regression Equations

Control Variables ↓	*Expected Signs of the Control Variables in Different Regression Equations*						
	CI	*CD*	*HYVR*	*FC*	*IG*	*LI*	*CAPI*
Farm Size	+/-	+/-	+/-	+/-	+/-		+
Extent of Irrigation	+	+	+	+	+		
Access to Extension	+	+	+	+/-			
Access to Finance	+	+	+	+	+		
Area under High-yielding Varieties	+/-						
Availability of Farm Labour	+	+/-					
Area under Fertiliser Intensive Crops				+			
Family Labour						+	
Area under Winter Paddy						-	
Locational characteristics	+/-	+/-	+/-	+/-	+/-	+/-	+/-

Source: Author.

RESULTS AND DISCUSSION OF EMPIRICAL ANALYSIS

Cropping Intensity

COMPARISON OF AVERAGE CROPPING INTENSITIES OF THE FARMS UNDER DIFFERENT TENURE STATUS

It is clear from Figure 5.1 that between the owner-operators and the pure tenants, cropping intensity is lower for the latter. In other

Figure 5.1. Owner-Operator and Pure Tenant (in %)

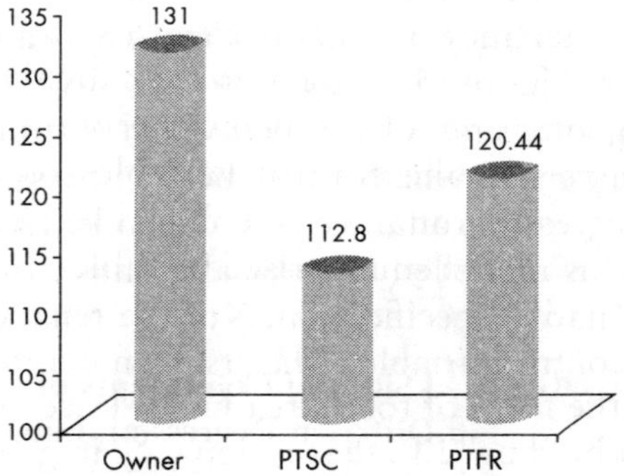

Notes: PTSC—pure tenant sharecropper; PTFR—pure tenant fixed rent.
Source: Author.

Figure 5.2. Owner-Operator Cum Tenant (in %)

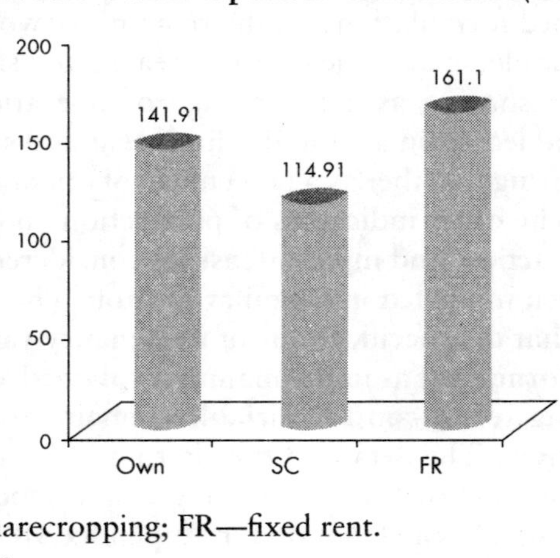

Notes: SC—sharecropping; FR—fixed rent.
Source: Author.

words, the pure tenants cultivate the land relatively less frequently. Again, within pure tenants, the value of the index of cropping intensity is further lower for sharecroppers as compared to the fixed rent tenants. A comparison of the cropping intensities of the owner operator-cum-tenant on her/his own land and leased-in land reveals that the farmer cultivates her/his leased-in land under fixed rent more frequently than her/his own land and sharecropped land. Thus, the impression that one gets from the figures is that tenancy in general (Figure 5.1) and sharecropping in particular (Figures 5.1 and 5.2) may have a negative impact on cropping intensity. What follows next is a multiple regression analysis to ascertain whether the above impression is indeed true.

In the regression analysis, the dependent variable cropping intensity (Y) is modelled as three alternative formulations, each having alternative specification(s) of the tenancy factor but the same set of control variables. The first formulation has the tenancy variable in the form of total area under lease as a percentage of operational holding (LI), that is, tenancy in general. The second formulation of the regression model has two specifications of the tenancy variables, which are area under sharecropping as a percentage of operational holding (SC) and area under fixed rent as a percentage of operational holding (FR). On the other hand, the third formulation has the remaining two forms of the tenancy variable, that is, leased-in area under sharecropping without cost sharing as a percentage of operational holding (SCWCS) and leased-in area under fixed rent and sharecropping with cost sharing together as a percentage of operational holding (FRSCCS). **The other indicators of production and productivity enhancing practices and input intensities considered in the study have also been modelled in a similar fashion. The only point to be noted is that the specifications of the tenancy variable change in different formulations in the manner explained above, but the corresponding set of control variables remains the same in all the formulations. The details of the alternative formulations and functional forms chosen for all the regression models and their justification have been elaborated in Appendix 5B.**

It may be mentioned here that the choice of the functional form for the regression model is guided by the nature of the dependent variable. In the context of cropping intensity, given the nature of the index, a left censored Tobit regression model has been formulated. The Maximum Likelihood estimates of the parameters have been obtained by using STATA 10.0. The estimated results of the regression analysis are summarised in Table 5.2.

Since the sample comprises of a cross-section of households, before estimating the models, the Breusch-Pagan test has been applied to check for the presence of heteroskedasticity in the data sets for all three formulations. The test shows the presence of heteroskedasticity. Subsequently, heteroskedasticity consistent robust standard errors have been estimated to take care of the problem (see Gujarati 2004). This exercise has been performed in the context of all other regression equations that would follow.

The results of the regression tally the impression that Figures 5.1 and 5.2 give. The coefficient of the first variant of the tenancy variable, that is, tenancy in general, is negative and significant at 10 per cent in formulation 1. Again, estimation of formulations 2 and 3 shows that two other variants of the tenancy variable, viz., the percentage of area under sharecropping and percentage of area under sharecropping without cost sharing, also have negative coefficients which are significant at 10 per cent. Thus, it can be inferred from the above results that tenancy in general and sharecropping in particular, especially sharecropping without cost sharing, have a negative and significant impact on cropping intensity. In other words, the tenant farmers, particularly the sharecroppers, tend to cultivate the land less frequently. The explanation for this finding may be found in the cropping patterns of the tenant farmers. The sharecroppers largely grow winter paddy whereas the fixed rent tenants lease-in land to grow crops like summer paddy, rape and mustard, and winter vegetables (see Table 4.13). While winter paddy is grown during the rainy season, the crops grown by the fixed rent tenants are usually rabi crops. Thus, it is evident that while the sharecroppers cultivate land during one part of the year, the fixed rent tenant does so in the other half of the year. This is why the cropping intensity of the tenant farmers is less. The fixed rent tenants, however, especially those who grow either of the following combinations of crops, viz., winter vegetable and rape and mustard, and summer paddy and rape and mustard, can cultivate at least some part of the land more than once even during one half of the year, since these are short duration crops. This is why the value of the index of cropping intensity is relatively higher for fixed rent tenants than for the sharecroppers.

Among the control variables, the coefficients of the extent of irrigation and all the location dummies are positive and significant in all three formulations of the model. The significance of the variable extent of irrigation speaks to the crucial role that irrigation plays in raising cropping intensity. Irrigation facilitates the cultivation of crops even during the rabi season. Besides, it allows for the raising of short duration crops and thereby frees the land for growing multiple crops. Thus, it is appropriate that irrigation has a positive and significant influence on cropping intensity. Again, the significance of all the locational dummies implies that the farmers in Morigaon, Nalbari, and Cachar cultivate their land more frequently as compared to those in the reference category, that is, Dibrugarh.

Table 5.2. Results of Left Censored Tobit Regression for Cropping Intensity

Versions ⟶	*Formulation 1*	*Formulation 2*	*Formulation 3*
Test of ⟶ *Heteroskedasticity*	*Breusch-Pagan test* *Chi*^{2} *[10] = 28.06* *Prob. = 0.0018* *Result: presence of heteroskedasticity*	*Breusch-Pagan test* *Chi*^{2} *[11] = 27.77* *Prob. = 0.0020* *Result: presence of heteroskedasticity*	*Breusch-Pagan test* *Chi*^{2} *[11] = 29.23* *Prob. = 0.0021* *Result: presence of heteroskedasticity*
Variables	*Estimates of coefficients/values*		
%OH Leased-in	–0.002* (0.001)		
%OH under SC		–0.002* (0.001)	
%OH under FR		–0.002 (0.002)	
%OH under SCWCS			–0. 003* (0.002)
%OH under FR+ SCCS			–0. 002 (0.001)
Farm Size	–0.012 (0.049)	–0.012 (0.049)	–0.011 (0.049)
Extent of Irrigation	0.005*** (0.001)	0.005*** (0.001)	0.005*** (0.001)

(contd.)

(Table 5.2 contd.)

Versions ⟶	*Formulation 1*	*Formulation 2*	*Formulation 3*
Test of ⟶ *Heteroskedasticity*	*Breusch-Pagan test* *Chi² [10] = 28.06* *Prob. = 0.0018* *Result: presence of heteroskedasticity*	*Breusch-Pagan test* *Chi² [11] = 27.77* *Prob. = 0.0020* *Result: presence of heteroskedasticity*	*Breusch-Pagan test* *Chi² [11] = 29.23* *Prob. = 0.0021* *Result: presence of heteroskedasticity*
Variables	*Estimates of coefficients/values*		
Access to Extension	–0.215	–0.215	–0.213
	(0.233)	(0.233)	(0.232)
Access to Finance	0.134	0.134	0.132
	(0.104)	(0.105)	(0.106)
% HYV Area	–0.002	–0.002	–0.002
	(0.002)	(0.002)	(0.002)
Farm Labour	0.007	0.007	0.009
	(0.035)	(0.035)	(0.035)
L_1	0.543***	0.543***	0.535***
	(0.157)	(0.158)	(0.161)
L_2	0.424**	0.424**	0.426**
	(0.165)	(0.165)	(0.164)
L_3	0.641***	0.642***	0.629***
	(0.13)	(0.132)	(0.134)
Constant	0.667***	0.667***	0.671***
	(0.185)	(0.185)	(0.186)
Pseudo R^2	0.1917	0.1917	0.1922
F	9.87***	9.00***	9.24***
	[10,210]	[11,209]	[11,209]

Notes: Figures within ( ) and [ ] are heteroskedasticity consistent robust standard error and degrees of freedom, respectively.
***, **, and * indicate significant at 1, 5, and 10 per cent, respectively
Source: Author.

Crop Diversification

COMPARISON OF THE AVERAGE VALUES OF THE INDEX OF CROP DIVERSIFICATION OF THE FARMERS UNDER DIFFERENT TENURE STATUS.

Figure 5.3 shows that the owner operators are more diversified than the pure tenants—both sharecroppers and fixed rent tenants. However, within the pure tenants, the value of the index measuring

Figure 5.3. Owner-operator and Pure Tenant

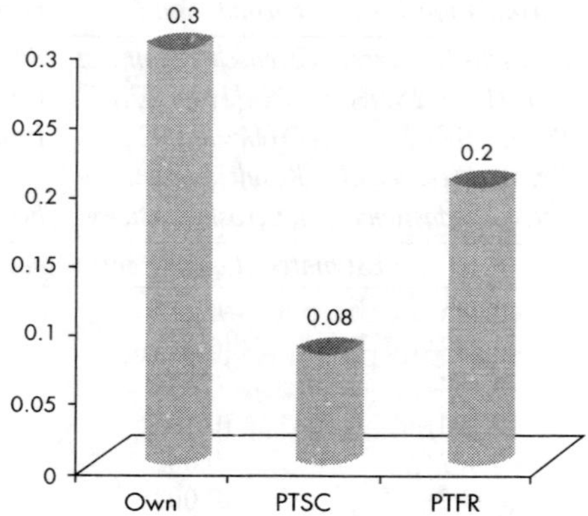

Notes: PTSC: pure tenant sharecropper; PTFR: pure tenant fixed rent.
Source: Author.

Figure 5.4. Owner Operator-Cum-Tenant

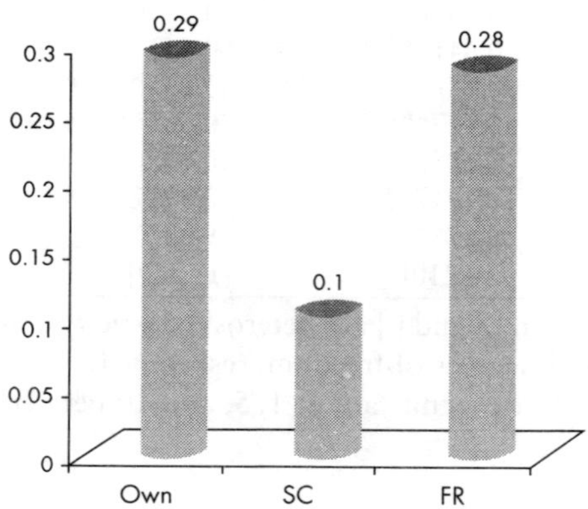

Notes: SC: sharecropping; FR: fixed rent.
Source: Author.

the extent of diversification is much lower for the shrecroppers. In the case of the owner operator-cum-tenant, the difference between the values of the index for own land (0.29) and for land leased-in under fixed rent (0.28) is not very pronounced. However, the extent of diversification is much lower on the sharecropped land of the owner operator-cum-tenant, as reflected in the value (0.1) of the index. Thus, the impression that one gets from Figures 5.3 and 5.4 is that tenant farmers in general and shrecroppers in particular are less diversified. A multiple regression model has been developed in the following to verify this preliminary impression.

The nature of the dependent variable, that is, the index of crop diversification, is such that a left censored Tobit regression model is considered appropriate in the present context. The Maximum Likelihood estimates of the parameters have been presented in Table 5.3.

Table 5.3. Results of Left Censored Tobit Regression for Crop Diversification

Versions ⟶	*Formulation 1*	*Formulation 2*	*Formulation 3*
Test of ⟶ *Heteroskedasticity*	*Breusch-Pagan test* Chi^2 *[9] = 4.70* *Prob. = 0.8599* *Result: no heteroskedasticity*	*Breusch-Pagan test* Chi^2 *[10] = 7.29* *Prob. = 0.6977* *Result: no heteroskedasticity*	*Breusch-Pagan test* Chi^2 *[10] = 8.43* *Prob. = 0.5871* *Result: no heteroskedasticity*
Variables	*Estimates of coefficients/values*		
%OH Leased in	–0.0013 ** (0.0006)		
%OH under SC		–0.002*** (0.0007)	
%OH under FR		–0.0001 (0.0008)	
%OH under SCWCS			–0.004*** (0.001)
%OH under FR+ SCCS			–0.0007 (0.0006)
Farm Size	0.043 (0.028)	0.043 (0.028)	0.044 (0.028)
Extent of Irrigation	0.002*** (0.0004)	0.002*** (0.0004)	0.001*** (0.0004)
Access to Extension	–0.203 (0.136)	–0.218 (0.135)	– 0.195 (0.134)

(contd.)

(Table 5.3 contd.)

Versions ⟶	*Formulation 1*	*Formulation 2*	*Formulation 3*
Test of ⟶ *Heteroskedasticity*	*Breusch-Pagan test* *Chi² [9] = 4.70* *Prob. = 0.8599* *Result: no heteroskedasticity*	*Breusch-Pagan test* *Chi² [10] = 7.29* *Prob. = 0.6977* *Result: no heteroskedasticity*	*Breusch-Pagan test* *Chi² [10] = 8.43* *Prob. = 0.5871* *Result: no heteroskedasticity*
Variables	*Estimates of coefficients/values*		
Access to Finance	0.119**	0.108*	0.111*
	(0.058)	(0.058)	(0.058)
Farm Labour	–0.001	–0.007	–0.003
	(0.012)	(0.02)	(0.02)
L_1	0.201***	0.183**	0.169**
	(0.071)	(0.071)	(0.072)
L_2	0.223***	0.226***	0.232***
	(0.07)	(0.069)	(0.069)
L_3	0.33***	0.36***	0.288***
	(0.068)	(0.069)	(0.069)
Constant	–0.075	–0.072	–0.058
	(0.104)	(0.103)	(0.103)
Pseudo R^2	0.2601	0.2763	0.2886
LR Chi^2	63.84***	67.82***	70.83***
	[9]	[10)	[10]

Notes: Figures within ( ) and [ ] are standard error and degrees of freedom, respectively.
***, **, and * indicate significant at 1, 5, and 10 per cent, respectively.
Source: Author.

The results of the regression analysis, as summarised in Table 5.3, show that the first variant of the tenancy variable, that is, tenancy in general, included in formulation 1 is significant at 5 per cent with a negative sign. Again, two other variants of the tenancy variable, viz., percentage of operational holding under sharecropping (in formulation 2) and percentage of operational holding under sharecropping without cost sharing (in formulation 3) also appear to be significant at 1 per cent with negative coefficients. These results imply that tenancy in general and sharecropping in particular, especially sharecropping without cost sharing, have a negative and significant impact on crop diversification. In other words, tenant farmers, especially the sharecroppers, are less diversified. The explanations provided to explain the lower value of the index of cropping intensity in the case of the tenants, especially the sharecroppers, hold good in the present context too.

Apart from tenancy, the extent of irrigation, access to finance, and all the locational dummies appear to be significant with positive signs in all three equations. Therefore, it may be inferred that irrigation contributes positively to crop diversification, and farmers with access to institutional credit are more diversified as compared to those who do not have access to institutional credit. Besides, farmers in the other three field study locations are more diversified as compared to those in the reference category, that is, Dibrugarh.

Extent of Adoption of High-Yielding Variety Rice

COMPARISON OF THE AVERAGE PROPORTION OF AREA UNDER HYVS IN RICE ACREAGES OF THE FARMERS UNDER DIFFERENT TENURE STATUS

Between the owner-operators and pure tenants, the fixed rent pure tenants devote a larger part of their total rice area to HYVs. Even the owner-operators devote a less amount of the total rice area

Figure 5.5. Owner-operator and Pure Tenant (in %)

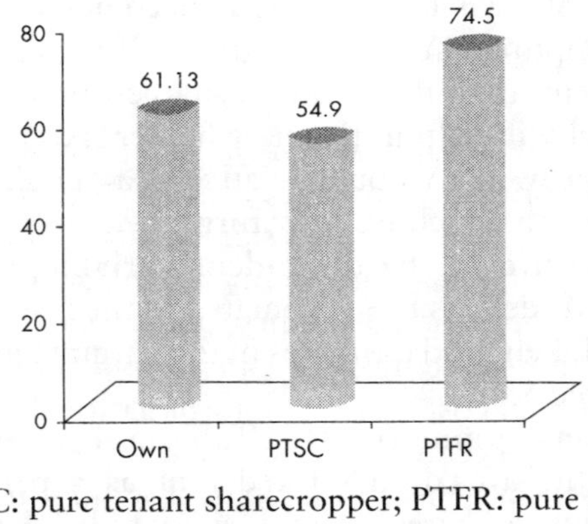

Notes: PTSC: pure tenant sharecropper; PTFR: pure tenant fixed rent.
Source: Author.

Figure 5.6. Owner Operator-Cum-Tenant (in %)

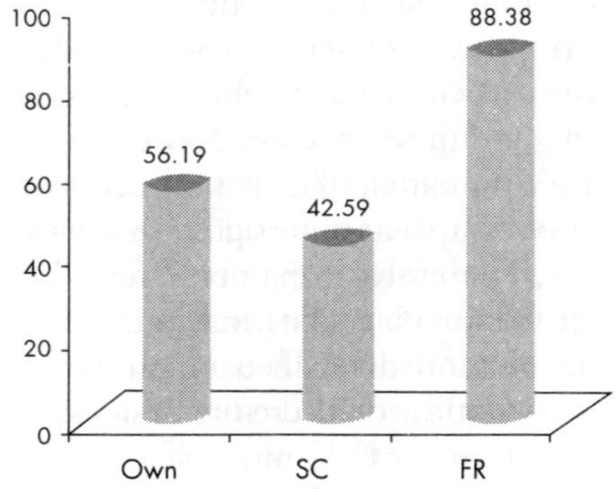

Notes: SC: sharecropping; FR: fixed rent.
Source: Author.

to HYVs as compared to the fixed rent pure tenants. As opposed to the 74.5 per cent of the total rice area devoted to HYVs by the fixed rent tenant, the owner-operators devote only 61.13 per cent. However, the extent of adoption of HYVs among the pure tenant sharecroppers is even lower than the owner-operators. A comparision of the extent of adoption of HYV rice by the owner operator-cum-tenant reveals that the farmer grows HYVs on as high as 88.38 per cent of the leased-in land under fixed rent, as opposed to only 42.59 per cent of the sharecropped area and 56.19 per cent of own land. Thus, it becomes clear that the likelihood of adopting HYVs rice is greater if the land is leased-in under fixed rent, than if it is under sharecropping. A mutiple regression model will help in testing whether fixed rent tenants indeed tend to grow HYVs on a relatively larger share of their total rice acreage, to which we now turn.

Given the nature of the dependent variable, a both side censored Tobit Model has been estimated in the present context. The Maximum Likelihood estimates of the parameters have been presented in Table 5.4.

The results, as summarised in Table 5.4, show that the coefficients of the area under fixed rent as a percentage of operational holding and area under fixed rent plus sharecropping with cost sharing as a percentage of operational holding in the second and third formulations of the regression model appear to be significant at 5 per cent and 10 per cent, respectively, bearing a positive sign. The coefficients of the remaining specifications of the tenancy variable are not significant. The results of the present exercise imply that although tenancy as such, or sharecropping in particular, does not inhibit the adoption of HYVs, on an average the fixed rent tenants and the sharecroppers leasing-in land under a cost-sharing arrangement devote a larger part of their rice acreages to HYVs relative to other farmers. The explanation as to why the above two groups of tenant farmers devote a comparatively higher share of their rice acreages to HYVs may be as follows. Insofar as the fixed rent tenants are concerned, while leasing-in land, they are guided by two considerations, viz., (*i*) output maximisation, and (*ii*) risk minimisation. Since they can retain the entire output that they produce, the fixed rent tenants have the incentive to maximise outputs from the leased-in land by supplying sufficient and better quality inputs. Guided by the objective of output maximisation, they devote a larger share of the leased-in land to growing HYVs, which fetch better returns compared to the traditional varieties. Again, to minimise risk (as has already been explained in Chapter 4), they usually grow summer paddy, which involves little weather risk. This last fact further incentivises fixed rent tenants to devote a larger share of their rice acreages to HYVs. On the other hand, the sharecroppers would not like to grow HYVs by bearing the entire cost burden, including that of other supplementary costly inputs, and then share the output equally with the lessors. Hence, only those sharecroppers leasing-in land under a cost-sharing arrangement devote a larger proportion of their rice acreages to growing HYVs.

Among the control variables, extent of irrigation, access to extension, access to finance, and all the locational dummies are significant. The coefficients of all these variables are positive and significant in all the formulations of the regression model. Thus, the results suggest that extent of irrigation, and access to extension service and finance contribute positively to the use of HYVs. Given the fact that HYVs fetch the best returns only when they are used in a supportive environment, provided by inputs like irrigation, technical guidance, and so on, the results

Table 5.4. Results of Both Side Censored Tobit Regression for Percentage of HYVs in Rice Acreages

Versions ⟶	*Formulation 1*	*Formulation 2*	*Formulation 3*
Test of ⟶ *Heteroskedasticity*	*Breusch-Pagan test* *Chi² [8] = 26.29* *Prob. = 0.0009* *Result: presence of heteroskedasticity*	*Breusch-Pagan test* *Chi² [9] = 26.49* *Prob. = 0.0017* *Result: presence of heteroskedasticity*	*Breusch-Pagan test* *Chi² [9] = 26.55* *Prob. = 0.0017* *Result: presence of heteroskedasticity*
Variables	*Estimates of coefficients/values*		
%OH Leased-in	0.113 (0.102)		
%OH under SC		–0.014 (0.119)	
%OH under FR		.38** (0.174)	
%OH under SCWCS			–0.085 (0.172)
%OH under FR+ SCCS			0.183* (0.114)
Farm Size	0.468 (4.232)	0.066 (4.216)	0.039 (4.184)
Extent of Irrigation	0.339** (0.15)	0. 318** (0.15)	0.322** (0.149)
Access to Extension	64.59** (24.86)	61.37** (24.72)	65.48** (24.87)
Access to Finance	24.54* (12.19)	21.5** (12.36)	23.52 ** (12.18)
L_1	118.01*** (17.19)	113.30*** (16.96)	114.64*** (17.07)
L_2	117.25*** (14.07)	115.82*** (13.91)	117.16*** (13.97)
L_3	60.96*** (11.97)	65.08*** (12.25)	55.86*** (12.61)
Constant	28.96** (13.24)	27.34** (12.95)	24.98** (13.38)
Pseudo R^2	0.1287	0.1316	0.1303
F	15.66*** [8,207]	14.25*** [9,206]	14.43*** [9,206]

Notes: Figures within ( ) and [ ] are heteroskedasticity consistent robust standard error and degrees of freedom, respectively.
***, **, and * indicate significant at 1, 5, and 10 per cent, respectively.
Source: Author.

of the estimated model are obvious. Again, with respect to the significance of the location dummies, it can be inferred that the average proportion of HYVs in the rice acreages of the farmers of the other three locations is higher than that of the farmers of the reference category, that is, Dibrugarh.

Fertiliser Consumption

COMPARISON OF THE AVERAGE AMOUNT OF NPK PER HECTARE APPLIED BY THE FARMS UNDER DIFFERENT TENURE STATUS

It is clear from Figure 5.7 that the fixed rent pure tenants apply more chemical fertilisers relative to the owner-operators and the pure tenant sharecroppers. Again, the owner operator-cum-tenant also applies more fertilisers on land leased-in under fixed rent as compared to the sharecropped land. In fact, the owner operator-cum-tenant uses more fertilisers on land leased-in under fixed rent than even on his own land. Thus, it apparently seems that fixed rent tenancy induces the farmers to apply more fertilisers. To verify the above preliminary finding, a multiple regression model has been developed in which NPK per hectare of gross cropped area is regressed on the independent variable tenancy and some other control variables.

A left censored Tobit model is considered appropriate in the present context, given the nature of the dependent variable. The Maximum Likelihood estimates of the parameters have been presented in Table 5.6.

The results of the regression analysis show that while coefficients of the third and fifth variants of the tenancy variable are significant, the remaining three are insignificant. The area under fixed rent as a percentage of operational holding in the second formulation of the model is significant at 5 per cent with a positive coefficient. Again, area under fixed rent plus area under sharecropping with cost sharing as a percentage of operational holding appears to have a positive and significant (at 10 per cent) coefficient in the third formulation. This implies that on the average, fixed rent tenants and those sharecroppers with whom the lessors share the cost of cultivation use more fertiliser (NPK per hectare) relative

Figure 5.7. Owner-operator and Pure Tenant (in kg)

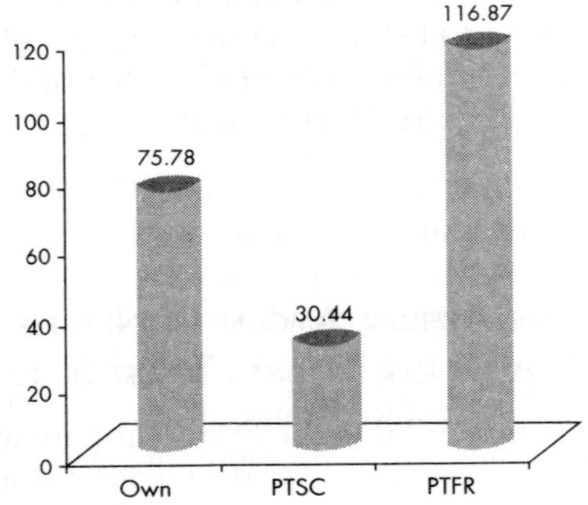

Notes: PTSC: pure tenant sharecropper; PTFR: pure tenant fixed rent.
Source: Author.

Figure 5.8. Owner Operator-Cum-Tenant (in kg)

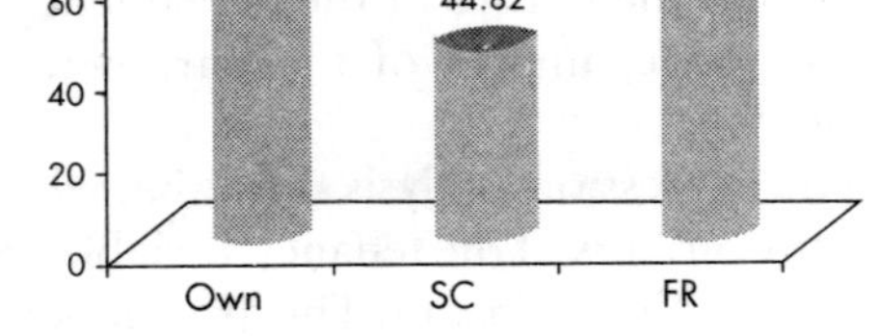

Notes: SC: sharecropping; FR: fixed rent.
Source: Author.

to other farmers. That the fixed rent tenants are inclined to use excessive amounts of fertiliser is further borne out by the numbers in Table 5.5. The table presents a comparison of the recommended level with the actual level of NPK applied on the owner-operated farms and on the plots under fixed rent tenancy in the case of the two most fertiliser-intensive crops, namely summer paddy and cabbage.[5] The figures in Table 5.5 show that both categories of farmers apply NPK at rates higher than the recommended dose. But while the applications by the owner operators exceed the recommended doses only marginally, the applications by fixed rent tenants are grossly excessive.[6] The excessive application of chemical fertiliser is surely not encouraging as far as soil health is concerned, and therefore may have adverse implications for the sustainable use of agricultural land.

Table 5.5. Comparison of Recommended Level of NPK with the Actual Level Applied by Owner-operators and Fixed Rent Tenants[7]

Ingredients of Fertiliser	*Summer Paddy (Kg/hectare)*			*Cabbage (Kg/hectare)*		
	Recommended	*Owner-operator*	*Fixed Rent Tenant*	*Recommended*	*Owner-operator*	*Fixed Rent Tenant*
N	40	55	98	120	107	216
P	20	28	32	60	101	105
K	20	9	10	60	46	54
NPK	80	93	140	240	254	374

Notes: (*i*) The source for the recommended level of NPK are Assam Agricultural University and Department of Agriculture, Government of Assam, 2009; (*ii*) the source for owner-operator and fixed rent tenant is the field survey data.
Source: Author.

The explanation for the liberal use of chemical fertiliser by fixed rent tenants is that they grow crops such as summer paddy, rape and mustard, and winter vegetables, which are in fact fertiliser-intensive crops. Besides, these crops are grown largely for commercial purposes, which further induce them to apply more fertilisers. Again, unlike those sharecroppers who bear the entire cost of cultivation by themselves, fixed rent tenants do not suffer from the incentive problem. Rather, they have all the incentive to supply the utmost possible efforts in terms of inputs and maximise the output. The short term of tenancy contracts may further strengthen the incentives to use fertilisers liberally.

The incentive problem does not influence those sharecroppers with whom the lessors share the costs of production either. The reason for this has already been explained while defining the fifth variant of the tenancy variable. This is probably why this category of sharecroppers also applies relatively more chemical fertilisers.

Among the control variables, the results show that farm size has a strong positive (significant at 1 per cent in all three formulations) impact on fertiliser consumption. The significant and positive coefficient of farm size implies that per hectare application of fertilisers by large farmers is greater relative to the small farmers. Again, the coefficient of the variable area under fertiliser-intensive crops (AFIC) is also positive and significant at 1 per cent in all three formulations. The other two variables which have positive and significant impacts on fertiliser use are extent of irrigation (IR) and access to finance (FIN). Thus, as expected, irrigation induces the use of fertilisers and farmers having access to institutional credit apply a relatively greater amount of fertilisers. Again, among the locational dummies, the dummy for Cachar is significant at 10 per cent and 5 per cent in the first and second formulations of the model, respectively, bearing a positive sign. This implies that farmers in this location

Table 5.6. Results of Left Censored Tobit Regression for NPK Per Hectare

Versions ⟶	*Formulation 1*	*Formulation 2*	*Formulation 3*
Test of ⟶ *Heteroskedasticity*	*Breusch-Pagan test* *Chi*^{2} *[9] = 54.74* *Prob. = 0.0000* *Result: presence of heteroskedasticity*	*Breusch-Pagan test* *Chi*^{2} *[10] = 78.04* *Prob. = 0.0000* *Result: presence of heteroskedasticity*	*Breusch-Pagan test* *Chi*^{2} *[10] = 69.95* *Prob. = 0.0000* *Result: presence of heteroskedasticity*
Variables	*Estimates of coefficients/values*		
%OH Leased-in	0.0015 (0.0016)		
%OH under SC		-0.002 (0.002)	
%OH under FR		0.006** (0.003)	

(contd.)

(Table 5.6 contd.)

Versions ⟶	*Formulation 1*	*Formulation 2*	*Formulation 3*
Test of ⟶ *Heteroskedasticity*	*Breusch-Pagan test* *Chi² [9] = 54.74* *Prob. = 0.0000* *Result: presence of heteroskedasticity*	*Breusch-Pagan test* *Chi² [10] = 78.04* *Prob. = 0.0000* *Result: presence of heteroskedasticity*	*Breusch-Pagan test* *Chi² [10] = 69.95* *Prob. = 0.0000* *Result: presence of heteroskedasticity*
Variables	*Estimates of coefficients/values*		
%OH under SCWCS			-0.0035 (0.0021)
%OH under FR+SCCS			0.003* (0.0018)
Farm Size	0.229*** (0.052)	0.224*** (0.05)	0.219*** (0.05)
Extent of Irrigation	0.006*** (0.002)	0.005*** (0.002)	0.006*** (0.002)
Access to Extension	-0.064 (0.287)	-0.105 (0.288)	-0.038 (0.277)
Access to Finance	0.262* (0.139)	0.234* (0.134)	0.26* (138)
%Area under FIC	0.012*** (0.002)	0.012*** (0.002)	0.012*** (0.003)
L_1	-0.212 (0.278)	-0.252 (0.273)	-.27 (0.28)
L_2	-0.422 (0.259)	-0.363 (0.245)	-0.381 (0.249)
L_3	0.327* (0.193)	0.448** (0.186)	-0.229 (0.200)
Constant	-0.728*** (0.168)	-0.649*** (0.161)	-0.628*** (0.164)
Pseudo R^2	0.1784	0.1948	0.1883
F	12.58*** [9, 209]	11.49*** [10, 208]	11.83*** [10, 208]

Notes: Figures within ( ) and [ ] are heteroskedasticity consistent robust standard error and degrees of freedom, respectively.
***, **, and * indicate significant at 1, 5, and 10 per cent, respectively.
Source: Author.

tend to apply more chemical fertilisers as compared to farmers in the reference category, that is, Dibrugarh.

Income Generated per Hectare of Operational Holding

Comparison of Average Income Generated per Hectare of Operational Holding from Cultivation by Households under Different Tenure Status

Figure 5.9. Owner-operator and Pure Tenant (in Rupees)

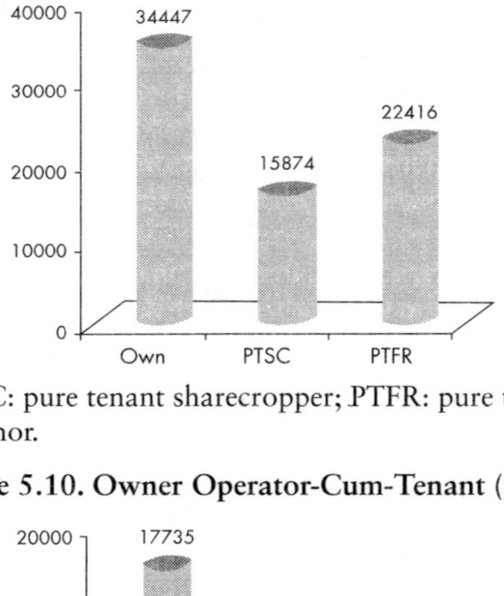

Notes: PTSC: pure tenant sharecropper; PTFR: pure tenant fixed rent.
Source: Author.

Figure 5.10. Owner Operator-Cum-Tenant (in Rupees)

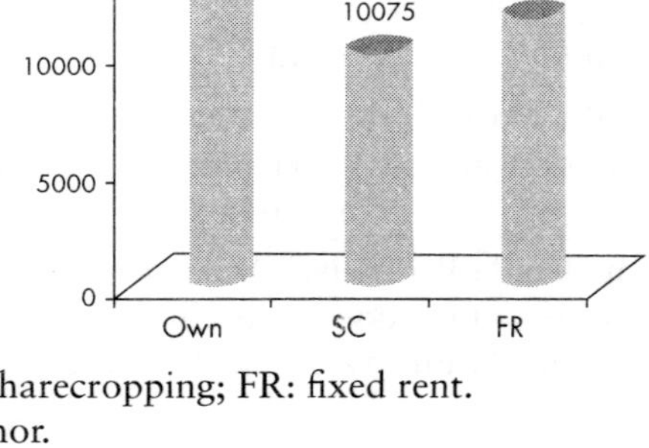

Notes: SC: sharecropping; FR: fixed rent.
Source: Author.

Figure 5.9 shows that owner-operator households generate more income per hectare of operational holding compared to the pure tenant households. Again, among the pure tenants, the fixed rent tenants generate more income per hectare of operational holding relative to the sharecroppers. In the case of the owner operator-cum-tenant, the farmer generates more income from her/his own land than from the leased-in land. Again, in the case of the leased-in land, income generated from the land leased-in under fixed rent is more than that from the sharecropped land. Thus, it is apparent that the income generated by tenant households, especially by the sharecroppers, is relatively less. To verify whether this apparent difference in per hectare income generation by farm households under different tenure status, as reflected in Figures 5.9 and 5.10, is indeed significant, an Ordinary Least Square multiple regression model has been developed. The estimates of the parameters have been summarised in Table 5.7.

The results summarised in Table 5.7 show that all variants of the tenancy variable, except the fourth, that is, area under sharecropping without cost sharing as a percentage of operational holding, are insignificant. The coefficient of the fourth variant is negative and significant at 5 per cent. It implies that on the average, the sharecroppers who lease-in land under no cost sharing arrangement generate less income per hectare of operational holding. The reason may be the fact that this group of farmers does not utilise the land efficiently. This inefficient utilisation of land is evident from the negative coefficient of this specification of the tenancy variable in the regression models for cropping intensity and crop diversification.

Among the control variables, extent of irrigation and access to finance appear to have a positive and significant impact on income generation. Households that have irrigation facilities on farm land and access to finance on an average generate more income per hectare of operational holding relative to other households without access to irrigation and finance. These households can cultivate lands frequently, diversify, and use HYVs, fertilisers, and other modern inputs, and thereby raise production and productivity and generate more income. Again, among the locational dummies, the dummy for Cachar is positive and significant at 1 per cent, implying that the farm households in this

Table 5.7. Results of Linear Regression for Income Generated Per Hectare of Operational Holding

Versions ⟶	*Formulation 1*	*Formulation 2*	*Formulation 3*
Test of Heteroskedasticity ⟶	*Breusch-Pagan test* Chi^2 *[7] = 64.11* *Prob. = 0.0000* *Result: presence of heteroskedasticity*	*Breusch-Pagan test* Chi^2 *[8] = 64.61* *Prob. = 0.0000* *Result: presence of heteroskedasticity*	*Breusch-Pagan test* Chi^2 *[8] = 64.17* *Prob. = 0.0000* *Result: presence of heteroskedasticity*
Variables	*Estimates of coefficients/values*		
%OH Leased in	– 60.64 (39.94)		
%OH under SC		– 64.68 (41.02)	
%OH under FR		– 54.87 (64.49)	
%OH under SCWCS			–98.67** (48.99)
%OH under FR+SCCS			–47.65 (45.73)
Farm Size	94.79 (1259.47)	87.55 (1265.55)	–3.38 (1262.29)
Extent of Irrigation	171.49** (69.53)	170.58** (69.31)	168.39** (69.52)
Access to Finance	9891.86** (4157.23)	9829.63** (4146.97)	9749.935** (4199.4)
L_1	7417.51 (6137.43)	7318.31 (6404.66)	6704.31 (6337.65)
L_2	–1544.69 (3965.6)	– 1569.17 (3990.04)	–1609.30 (3983.82)
L_3	14140.37*** (3935.89)	14238.53*** (3983.49)	13138.24*** (4283.98)
Constant	27317.78*** (3929.32)	27381.97*** (3927.61)	28155.79*** (4094.74)
R^2	0.3267	0.3267	0.3288
F	8.84*** [7,207]	8.27*** [8,206]	10.10*** [8,206]

Notes: Figures within ( ) and [ ] are robust standard error and degrees of freedom, respectively.
*** and **, indicate significant at 1 and 5 per cent, respectively.
Source: Author.

location generate more income compared to the farm households in the reference category, that is, Dibrugarh.

Labour Intensity

COMPARISON OF THE AVERAGE LABOUR INTENSITIES OF FARM HOUSEHOLD UNDER DIFFERENT TENURE STATUS

Figure 5.11. Owner-operator and Pure Tenant (in Rupees)

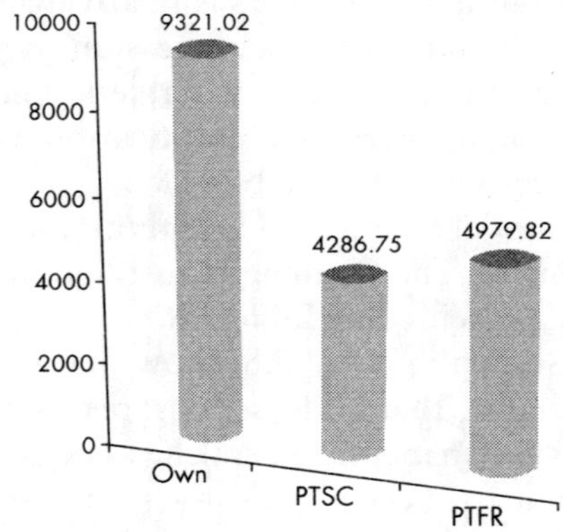

Notes: PTSC: pure tenant sharecropper; PTFR: pure tenant fixed rent.
Source: Author.

Figure 5.12. Owner Operator-Cum-Tenant (in Rupees)

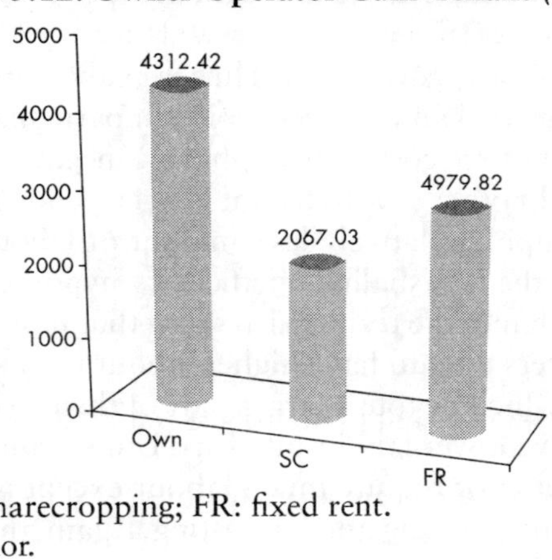

Notes: SC: sharecropping; FR: fixed rent.
Source: Author.

Figure 5.11 shows that the labour intensity of the owner-operators is substantially higher than that of the pure tenants. Again, within the pure tenants, the fixed rent tenants have slightly higher labour intensity compared to the sharecroppers. In the case of the owner operator-cum-tenants, the farmer applies more labour on his own land than on the leased-in land. However, the labour intensity of the owner operator-cum-tenant on the land leased-in under fixed rent is slightly higher than that on the sharecropped land. Thus, the picture emerging out of Figures 5.11 and 5.12 is that the labour intensity of tenant farmers is relatively less. To verify the above impression statistically, a regression model has been formulated in which the dependent variable labour intensity is modelled as a function of alternative specifications of the tenancy factor alongside some control variables.

The regression model formulated for labour intensity is of the form of semi-log linear. The Ordinary Least Square estimates of the parameters are presented in Table 5.8.

The results, as shown in Table 5.8, show that the first variant of the tenancy variable, that is, leased-in area as percentage of operational holding or tenancy in general, has a negative coefficient which is significant at 1 per cent. Again, the second specification of the tenancy variable—area under sharecropping as a percentage of operational holding—is significant with a negative sign at 1 per cent in the second formulation of the model. The fourth specification of the tenancy variable is also significant at 1 per cent in the third formulation. The coefficient of the fourth form of the tenancy variable also takes a negative sign. Thus, the above results imply that tenancy in general and sharecropping in particular, especially sharecropping without cost sharing, have a negative impact on labour intensity. In other words, tenant farmers, and especially the sharecroppers, supply relatively less amount of labour. This is in conformity with the Marshallian inefficiency hypothesis.

On the other hand, the results also show that households with more farm workers tend to have higher labour intensity. Further, the households which devote a larger part of their rice acreage to winter paddy have lower labour intensity. Unlike summer paddy, winter paddy does not require much labour except for the usual work, such as transplanting and harvesting. Again, the locational

Table 5.8. Results of Semi Log-Linear Regression Analysis for Labour Intensity

Versions ⟶	*Formulation 1*	*Formulation 2*	*Formulation 3*
Test of ⟶ *Heteroskedasticity*	*Breusch-Pagan test* *Chi² [6] = 53.43* *Prob. = 0.0000* *Result: presence of heteroskedasticity*	*Breusch-Pagan test* *Chi² [7] = 53.46* *Prob. = 0.0000* *Result: presence of heteroskedasticity*	*Breusch-Pagan test* *Chi² [7] = 53.68* *Prob. = 0.0000* *Result: presence of heteroskedasticity*
Variables	*Estimates of coefficients/values*		
%OH Leased-in	–0.0016*** (0.0006)		
%OH under SC		–0.002*** (0.0006)	
%OH under FR		–0.0005 (0.001)	
%OH under SCWCS			–0.003*** (0.001)
%OH under FR+SCCS			–0.001 (0.0007)
Family Labour	0.00005*** (0.00001)	0.00005*** (0.00001)	0.00005*** (0.00001)
Area under Winter Paddy	–0.0036*** (0.0009)	–0.003*** (0.0009)	–0.003*** (0.0009)
L_1	0.1115 (0.092)	0.105 (0.094)	0.098 (0.093)
L_2	0.029 (0.081)	0.029 (0.082)	0.033 (0.08)
L_3	0.186** (0.072)	0.209*** (0.073)	0.149* (0.077)
Constant	8.99*** (0.105)	8.96*** (0.106)	8.98*** (0.103)
R^2	0.2028	0.2107	0.2177
F	8.89*** [6, 211]	9.27*** [7, 210]	8.8*** [7, 210]

Notes: Figures within ( ) and [ ] are robust standard error and degrees of freedom, respectively.

***, **, and * indicate significant at 1, 5, and 10 per cent, respectively.

Source: Author.

dummies for Morigaon and Cachar appear to be positive and significant at 1 per cent in all three formulations, implying that the farmers in these two locations have higher labour intensity as compared to those in the reference category, that is, Dibrugarh.

CAPITAL INTENSITY

Comparison of the Average Capital Intensities of the Farm Households under Different Tenure Status.

Figure 5.13 shows that the capital intensities of the owner-operators are higher than that of the pure tenants. Contrary to the findings in all the previous sections, the pure tenant sharecroppers have higher capital intensities than the fixed rent pure tenants. In the case of an owner operator-cum-tenant, as shown in Figure 5.14, the tenant's capital expenditure per hectare of gross cropped area is more on her/his own land than on the leased-in land. However, capital intensity is slightly higher on the land leased-in under fixed rent than on sharecropped land. Thus, Figures 5.13 and 5.14 fail to give any clear impression of whether tenancy in general and any of its forms in particular may have an impact

Figure 5.13. Owner-operator and Pure Tenant (in Rupees)

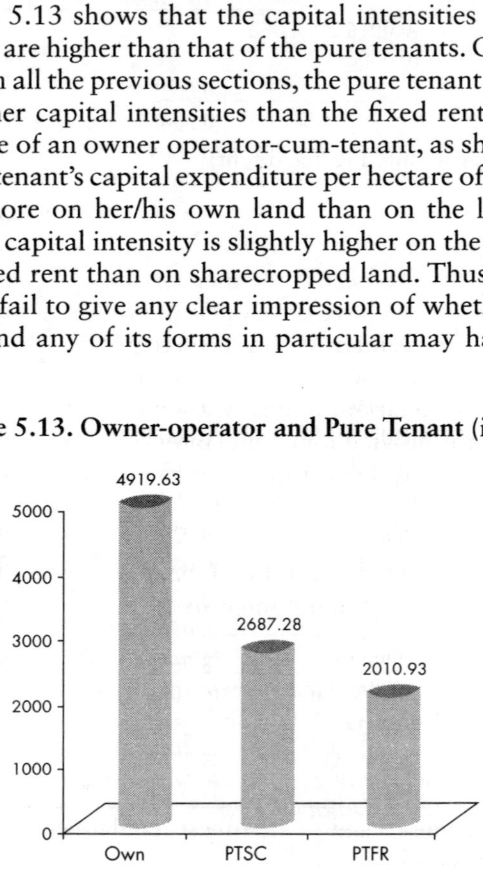

Notes: PTSC: pure tenant sharecropper; PTFR: pure tenant fixed rent.
Source: Author.

Figure 5.14. Owner Operator-Cum-Tenant (in Rupees)

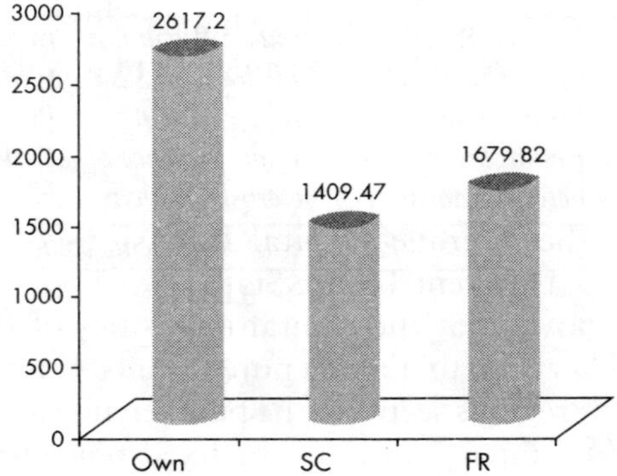

Notes: SC: sharecropping; FR: fixed rent.
Source: Author.

on capital intensity. To verify whether tenancy has any impact on capital intensity, we have developed the following regression model in which capital intensity has been regressed on alternative specifications of the tenancy variable and certain control variables.

Like in the case of labour intensity, a semi-log linear regression model has been formulated for capital intensity. Table 5.9 presents the Ordinary Least Square estimates of the parameters.

Table 5.9. Results of Semi Log-Linear Regression for Capital Intensity

Versions ⟶	*Formulation 1*	*Formulation 2*	*Formulation 3*
Test of ⟶ *Heteroskedasticity*	*Breusch-Pagan test Chi² [5] = 17.31 Prob. = 0.0040 Result: presence of heteroskedasticity*	*Breusch-Pagan test Chi² [6] = 20.32 Prob. = 0.0024 Result: presence of heteroskedasticity*	*Breusch-Pagan test Chi² [6] = 17.59 Prob. = 0.0073 Result: presence of heteroskedasticity*
Variables	*Estimates of coefficients/values*		
%OH Leased-in	–0.00002 (0.0006)		

(contd.)

(Table 5.9 contd.)

Versions ⟶	*Formulation 1*	*Formulation 2*	*Formulation 3*
Test of ⟶ *Heteroskedasticity*	*Breusch-Pagan test* *Chi*^{2} *[5] = 17.31* *Prob. = 0.0040* *Result: presence of heteroskedasticity*	*Breusch-Pagan test* *Chi*^{2} *[6] = 20.32* *Prob. = 0.0024* *Result: presence of heteroskedasticity*	*Breusch-Pagan test* *Chi*^{2} *[6] = 17.59* *Prob. = 0.0073* *Result: presence of heteroskedasticity*
Variables		*Estimates of coefficients/values*	
%OH under SC		–0.0007 (0.0006)	
%OH under FR		0.001 (0.001)	
%OH under SCWCS			–0.00037 (0.0008)
%OH under FR+SCCS			0.0001 (0.0006)
Farm Size	0.068*** (0.023)	0.065*** (0.023)	0.066*** (0.024)
L_1	0.229*** (0.064)	0.20*** (0.064)	0.219*** (0.063)
L_2	0.088 (0.059)	0.085 (0.06)	0.088 (0.059)
L_3	0.330*** (0.057)	0.35*** (0.06)	0.321*** (0.058)
Constant	8.08*** (0.064)	8.08*** (0.063)	8.08*** (0.065)
R^2	0.1466	0.1583	0.1475
F	7.95*** [5, 212]	7.31*** [6, 211]	6.60*** [6, 211]

Notes: Figures within ( ) and [ ] are robust standard error and degrees of freedom, respectively.
*** indicate significant at 1 per cent.
Source: Author.

The results shown in Table 5.9 suggest that tenancy as such does not have any impact on the capital intensity of the farmers. None of the specifications of the tenancy variable appears to be significant in any of the three formulations of the regression model. However, the coefficient of the variable farm size is positive and significant at 1 per cent in all three formulations. This implies that capital intensity is rather a function of farm size, and larger farms tend to be more capital intensive. Among the locational dummies, the dummies for Morigaon and Cachar are significant at 1 per cent with positive signs in all three formulations, implying that the farmers in these locations are more capital intensive than those in the reference category, that is, Dibrugarh.

SUMMARY OF THE FINDINGS

The results of the empirical analysis show that tenancy in general and sharecropping in particular, especially sharecropping without cost sharing arrangement, have a very significant adverse impact on cropping intensity and crop diversification. Further, it has been found that the sharecroppers who lease-in land under no cost sharing arrangement generate less income per hectare of operational holding relative to other farmers. On the other hand, the results of the analysis reveal that the fixed rent tenants devote a larger part of their rice acreages to HYVs and use more chemical fertilisers (NPK per hectare) than even the owner-operators. **The liberal application of chemical fertilisers by the fixed rent tenants may have adverse implications for the sustainable use of agricultural land.**

Insofar as input intensities are concerned, tenancy in general and sharecropping in particular are found to have a negative impact on labour intensity. **Thus, it may be concluded that the results of the present analysis are largely in conformity with the Marshallian theoretical debate, that is, the sharecroppers are relatively inefficient.**

NOTES

1. Net income generated could not be calculated due to insufficient information for estimating depreciation of agricultural capital goods.
2. The market value of a crop is given by the product of the total crop output and the average price received by sample farmers selling the crop in their respective localities.

3. This, however, applies only to the observable inputs. For a detailed discussion on this issue, see Ray (1998).

4. Apart from tenancy, some other variables may influence the indicators of production and productivity enhancing practices and input intensities of a farm. In order to isolate the effect of tenancy and its various forms on these indicators, the impacts of these variables have to be controlled for. These variables have been identified from the existing literature.

5. In the present context, the recommended level of NPK refers to the minimum dose of NPK that maximises the return/yield in a round of cultivation. However, it is not necessary that the recommended level of NPK also be the optimal level for soil health. Nevertheless, it is instructive to compare the recommended level with the actual level of NPK to infer the fertiliser utilisation pattern of the farmers, and understanding its implications for soil health. A very high level of NPK as compared to the recommended level is very likely to have adverse implications for soil health.

6. It can also be observed from Table 5.5 that neither owner-operators nor the fixed rent tenants apply NPK in the recommended proportion. The application of NPK in an imbalanced proportion may be a fallout of the price distortions that stem from the subsidy given to the farmers, especially for urea.

7. The overall application of NPK, as shown in Figures 5.7 and 5.8 (for all crops together), is lower as compared to the use of NPK in summer paddy and cabbage, as the other crops that the farmers grow are not very fertiliser-intensive. For example, chemical fertiliser is rarely used in the cultivation of winter paddy, to which the farmers devote a substantial portion of the cropped area.

Appendix 5A

Justifications for the Expected Sign of the Control Variables used in Different Regression Models

Cropping Intensity

Farm Size (FS): Usually, smaller farms are expected to cultivate the land more frequently since they possess relatively more labour but less land. However, a counter-argument states that a small farm may face constraints on resources other than labour, and hence may be unable to raise crops frequently. Therefore, the sign of the coefficient of this variable cannot be anticipated *a priori*.

Extent of Irrigation (IR): Irrigation facilitates the cultivation of short duration crops and thereby allows the raising of multiple crops during a year. Hence, it may be expected that cropping intensity will be more on irrigated land, relative to non-irrigated land. In other words, cropping intensity should have a positive relation with the extent of irrigation.

Access to Extension (EXT): Extension services play an important role in spreading awareness and knowledge about new technologies and superior methods of cultivation. Farmers receiving suggestions or knowledge about better crop varieties, application of various inputs, and so on are likely to cultivate land more frequently. Thus, the coefficient of the variable should bear a positive sign.

Access to Finance (FIN): If a farmer has access to institutional credit, her/his ability to purchase inputs like fertilisers, diesel for irrigation, tractor time, and so on will improve. This may increase the likelihood of raising multiple crops. Thus, access to finance should induce cropping intensity.

Area under High-yielding Varieties (PHYV): High-yielding varieties usually mature in a relatively shorter period of time and thereby free up the land for another crop. Hence, it may be assumed that if HYVs are grown on more land, the gross cropped areas will also be more; in other words, cropping intensity will be higher. However, there are empirical instances (Bezbaruah and Roy 2002) where the relation between the area under HYVs and cropping intensity has been found to be otherwise. Hence, the sign of the coefficient of this variable cannot be anticipated *a priori*.

Availability of Farm Labour (FL): Availability of farm labour may help a household to raise crops more frequently in a year. Moreover, the presence of a greater number of farm workers in a household may put pressure on the household to create employment opportunities for them, and consequently, to cultivate the land more frequently. Thus, a positive relation between farm labour and cropping intensity is expected.

Locational Characteristics: How agro-climatic variations would impact cropping intensity is an empirical question. Hence, the signs of the coefficients of the dummy variables cannot be predicted *a priori*.

CROP DIVERSIFICATION

Farm Size (FS): The relationship between farm size and crop diversification is a matter for empirical investigation. Usually small farms with abundant farm labour may diversify and cultivate multiple crops. But they face constraints on financial resources when it comes to buying improved technologies, more capital, etc., which are inevitable for diversification towards high-value crops (Birthal, et al. 2006). Again, according to a study by Pope and Prescott (1980), a larger farm may specialise in one crop if it is associated with economies of scale. However, in the absence of such economies of scale, and if the farm is risk averse, it will diversify even if it is a large one.

Extent of Irrigation (IR): Irrigation is an important determinant of the pattern and speed of crop diversification, especially in the rain-fed areas. In the rain-fed region, agricultural lands usually remain fallow during the rabi season. Irrigation facilitates cultivation during the rabi season as well, and thereby allows the farm households to diversify. Thus, irrigation should have a positive relationship with crop diversification.

Access to Extension (EXT): The farmers who have benefited from extension services should be in an advantageous position to diversify. Hence, the coefficient of the variable should bear a positive sign.

Access to Finance (FIN): The greater the number of crops grown, the larger is the financial requirement, especially when the farmers diversify towards high-value crops. Therefore, access to finance should influence the extent of diversification positively.

Availability of Farm Labour (FL): Availability of farm labour may allow the farm household to diversify and grow more crops. However, if farm labour is too abundant, the household may cultivate the staple crop in order to ensure food security. Hence, the sign of the coefficient of this variable cannot be anticipated *a priori*.

Locational Characteristics: The signs of the coefficients of the dummy variables cannot be predicted *a priori*.

EXTENT OF ADOPTION OF HIGH-YIELDING VARIETY RICE

Farm Size (FS): Usually the adoption of HYVs rice is scale neutral, barring of course those farms which are too small in size and hence non-viable. Hence, *a priori* it is difficult to say whether the large farmers or small farmers will use HYVs to a greater extent. However, since the use of HYVs has to be complemented by other costly inputs like chemical fertilisers and irrigation, one may expect large farmers to devote a larger part of their rice acreages to HYVs. Thus, whether farm size has a positive or negative impact on the use of HYVs in the context of our study largely remains an empirical question to be investigated.

Extent of Irrigation (IR): It is a well-known fact that HYVs fetch the best returns only when they are supported by irrigation. Hence, we expect irrigation to have a positive impact on the extent of adoption of HYVs.

Access to Extension (EXT): Farmers who have contact with extension workers and who received technical guidance from them on how to grow the HYVs are likely to devote a larger share of rice acreages to HYVs. Thus, we expect the coefficient of the variable to bear a positive sign.

Access to Finance (FIN): As has already been mentioned, the HYVs fetch higher returns only when they are used along with other inputs like fertilisers, irrigation, etc. These inputs are costly, and hence require financial resources. Thus, it may be expected that the farmers who have access to institutional credit may use HYVs on a larger part of their rice acreages.

Locational Characteristics: The signs of the coefficients of the dummy variables cannot be predicted *a priori*.

FERTILISER CONSUMPTION

Farm Size (FS): *A priori* there is no reason why a small or a large farmer should apply a greater or less amount of NPK per hectare than the other. However, given the perceived financial resource constraint faced by the small farms, the extent of fertiliser application by them may be relatively less. Hence, the sign of the coefficient of this variable cannot be anticipated *a priori*.

Extent of Irrigation (IR): Irrigation is usually considered a precondition for the use of fertilisers as it leads to better absorption of fertilisers. Hence, it is expected that irrigation will induce the application of fertilisers, and therefore the coefficient of the variable will take a positive sign.

Access to Extension (EXT): We expect the farmers who have benefited from the extension service network to make judicious use of fertilisers, which may be more or less than that used by the farmers on their own. Thus, whether access to extension services induces the farmers to use more or less fertilisers is again a question of empirical investigation.

Access to Finance (FIN): It may be expected that the coefficient of this variable will take a positive sign, as purchasing fertilisers requires financial resources. Thus, a farmer with access to finance may use a greater amount of fertiliser compared to a farmer who does not have access to finance.

Area under Fertiliser-Intensive Crops (AFIC): It is obvious that fertiliser consumption will be more if a farmer grows fertiliser-intensive crops on a larger part of his operational holding. Hence, the coefficient of this variable should bear a positive sign.

Locational Characteristics: The signs of the coefficients of the dummy variables cannot be predicted *a priori*.

INCOME GENERATED

Farm Size (FS): While on the one hand the small farms may have the advantage of abundant labour, which helps in raising many crops and consequently the income, they may face constraints on financial resources on the other. Big farms, however, usually do not have financial constraints, but may confront managerial problems. Hence, the sign of the coefficient of this variable cannot be anticipated *a priori*.

Extent of Irrigation (IR): Irrigation has a significant positive impact on the production and productivity enhancing practices. It is therefore obvious to expect that irrigation will influence the generation of income positively.

Access to Finance (FIN): Access to finance should influence the generation of income positively by facilitating the use of modern inputs.

Locational Characteristics: The signs of the coefficients of the dummy variables cannot be predicted *a priori*.

LABOUR INTENSITY

Family labour (FL): It may be expected that a household with more farm workers will also have a higher labour intensity.

Area under Winter Paddy (AWP): Winter rice is the predominant crop grown in Assam. In the context of our sample, too, it has been found that about 60 per cent of the gross cropped area is under winter paddy. During the course of the field visit, it was observed that farmers apply a relatively less amount of all inputs while growing winter paddy. The reason may be the fact that winter paddy is grown during the rainy season and is subjected to weather risk. As a result, farmers may not like to apply certain inputs like fertilisers in large quantities. Besides, it does not require irrigation, and consequently the requirement for applying other inputs, including labour, is also reduced. Hence, *a priori*, it may be expected that the higher the share of winter paddy in the total cropped area, the lower will be the labour intensity.

Locational characteristics: The signs of the coefficients of the dummy variables cannot be predicted *a priori*.

CAPITAL INTENSITY

Farm Size (FS): It may be expected that capital intensity will vary positively with farm size. Large farmers with more financial resources may tend to be more capital intensive.

Locational characteristics: The signs of the coefficients of the dummy variables cannot be predicted *a priori*.

Appendix 5B

Functional Forms Chosen for Different Regression Models

Cropping Intensity

The value of the dependent variable, that is, the index of cropping intensity, is either 100 or any value greater than 100. This implies that the lower end of the value of the dependent variable is 100, with no limit for the upper end. In our data set, there are 98 farmers for whom the value of the index of cropping intensity is 100. Thus, we have a cluster of observations at 100. In such a situation, a linear regression is not appropriate; rather, a Tobit model with censoring at the lower (left) end will be a better technique.

The Tobit model is formulated with the help of latent variable Y_i^* which may take any probable value, but is not always observable. Thus, in the context of the three formulations of the model, Y_i^* has been formulated in the following manner.

$$Y_i^* = \beta_0 + \beta_1 LI_i + \beta_2 FS_i + \beta_3 IR_i + \beta_4 EXT_i + \beta_5 FIN_i + \beta_6 PHYV_i + \beta_7 FL_i + \beta_8 L_{1i} + \beta_9 L_{2i} + \beta_{10} L_{3i} + U_i \quad \text{.. (5B.1)}$$

$$Y_i^* = \beta_0 + \beta_1 SC_i + \beta_2 FR_i + \beta_3 FS_i + \beta_4 IR_i + \beta_5 EXT_i + \beta_6 FIN_i + \beta_7 PHYV_i + \beta_8 FL_i + \beta_9 L_{1i} + \beta_{10} L_{2i} + \beta_{11} L_{3i} + U_i \quad \text{.. (5B.2)}$$

$$Y_i^* = \beta_0 + \beta_1 SCWCS_i + \beta_2 FRSCCS_i + \beta_3 FS_i + \beta_4 IR_i + \beta_5 EXT_i + \beta_6 FIN_i + \beta_7 PHYV_i + \beta_8 FL_i + \beta_9 L_{1i} + \beta_{10} L_{2i} + \beta_{11} L_{3i} + U_i \quad \text{.. (5B.3)}$$

Where, U_is are the random disturbances which are assumed to be normally distributed with zero mean.

The observed dependent variable Y_i is linked to the latent variable Y_i^* as per the following formulation:

$$Y_i = 100 \text{ for } Y_i^* < 100$$
$$= Y_i^* \text{ for } Y_i^* \geq 100$$

CROP DIVERSIFICATION

The dependent variable being bounded between 0 and 1, a linear regression model is not suitable as the predicted value from a linear regression will not necessarily be contained within the interval of 0 and 1. Again, we see a cluster of 76 observations at the lower end in which the dependent variable takes the value 0. Hence, a censored Tobit model with censoring at the lower end will be appropriate in the present context.

The Tobit model is formulated with the help of latent variable Y_i^* which may take any probable value, but is not always observable. Thus, Y_i^* has been formulated to accommodate the three formulations of the model in the following manner.

$$Y_i^* = \beta_0 + \beta_1 LI_i + \beta_2 FS_i + \beta_3 IR_i + \beta_4 EXT_i + \beta_5 FIN_i + \beta_6 FL_i + \beta_7 L_{1i} + \beta_8 L_{2i} + \beta_9 L_{3i} + U_i \quad \text{.......} (5B.4)$$

$$Y_i^* = \beta_0 + \beta_1 SC_i + \beta_2 FR_i + \beta_3 FS_i + \beta_4 IR_i + \beta_5 EXT_i + \beta_6 FIN_i + \beta_7 FL_i + \beta_8 L_{1i} + \beta_9 L_{2i} + \beta_{10} L_{3i} + U_i \quad \text{.......} (5B.5)$$

$$Y_i^* = \beta_0 + \beta_1 SCWCS_i + \beta_2 FRSCCS_i + \beta_3 FS_i + \beta_4 IR_i + \beta_5 EXT_i + \beta_6 FIN_i + \beta_7 FL_i + \beta_8 L_{1i} + \beta_9 L_{2i} + \beta_{10} L_{3i} + U_i \quad \text{.......} (5B.6)$$

Where, U_is are the random disturbances which are assumed to be normally distributed with zero mean.

The observed dependent variable Y_i is linked to the latent variable Y_i^* as per the following formulation:

$$Y_i = 0 \text{ for } Y_i^* < 0$$
$$= Y_i^* \text{ for } 0 \leq Y_i^* \leq 1$$

EXTENT OF ADOPTION OF HIGH-YIELDING VARIETY RICE

The dependent variable is such that it takes values within the range of 0 to 100 per cent. For a farmer who does not grow HYVs at all, the value of the dependent variable is 0, whereas it is 100 when the farmer uses HYVs in his entire rice acreages. Since the dependent variable is bounded between 0 and 100, a linear regression model is not suitable as the predicted value from a linear regression will not necessarily be contained within the interval of 0 and 100. Again, as per the above formulation of the dependent variable, we see clusters of observations at both ends in which the dependent variable takes the values 0 and 100, respectively. There are 44 observations for which the value of the dependent variable is 0, and in the case of another 82 observations, the dependent variable takes the value of 100. Hence, in the present context, a censored Tobit model with censoring at both ends will be appropriate.

The Tobit model is formulated with the help of latent variable Y_i^* which may take any probable value, but is not always observable. Thus, Y_i^* has been formulated in the following manner for each of the three formulations.

$$Y_i^* = \beta_0 + \beta_1 LI_i + \beta_2 FS_i + \beta_3 IR_i + \beta_4 EXT_i + \beta_5 FIN_i + \beta_6 L_{1i} + \beta_7 L_{2i} + \beta_8 L_{3i} + U \quad \text{..........} \quad (5B.7)$$

$$Y_i^* = \beta_0 + \beta_1 SC_i + \beta_2 FR_i + \beta_3 FS_i + \beta_4 IR_i + \beta_5 EXT_i + \beta_6 FIN_i + \beta_7 L_{1i} + \beta_8 L_{2i} + \beta_9 L_{3i} + U_i \quad \text{..........} \quad (5B.8)$$

$$Y_i^* = \beta_0 + \beta_1 SCWCS_i + \beta_2 FRSCCS_i + \beta_3 FS_i + \beta_4 IR_i + \beta_5 EXT_i + \beta_6 FIN_i + \beta_7 L_{1i} + \beta_8 L_{2i} + \beta_9 L_{3i} + U_i \quad \text{..........} \quad (5B.9)$$

Where, U_is are the random disturbances which are assumed to be normally distributed with zero mean.

The observed dependent variable Y_i is linked to the latent variable Y_i^* as per the following formulation:

$$\begin{aligned} Y_i &= 0 \text{ for } Y_i^* < 0 \\ &= Y_i^* \text{ for } 0 \le Y_i^* \le 100 \\ &= 100 \text{ for } Y^* > 100 \end{aligned}$$

FERTILISER CONSUMPTION

The value that the dependent variable, that is, NPK per hectare, takes is either 0 or any value greater than 0. For the farmers who do not apply chemical fertilisers at all, the value of the dependent variable is 0. This implies that the lower end of the value of the dependent variable is 0, with no limit for the upper end. In our data set, there are 43 farmers for whom the value of the dependent variable is 0. Thus, we have a cluster of observations at 0. In such a situation, a linear regression is not appropriate; rather, a Tobit model with censoring at the lower (left) end will be a better technique.

The Tobit model is formulated with the help of the latent variable Y_i^* which may take any probable value, but is not always observable. Thus, in the context of the three formulations of the model, Y_i^* has been formulated in the following manner.

$$Y_i^* = \beta_0 + \beta_1 LI_i + \beta_2 FS_i + \beta_3 IR_i + \beta_4 EXT_i + \beta_5 FIN_i + \beta_6 AFIC_i + \beta_7 L_{1i} + \beta_8 L_{2i} + \beta_9 L_{3i} + U_i \quad \text{..............................} (5B.10)$$

$$Y_i^* = \beta_0 + \beta_1 SC_i + \beta_2 FR_i + \beta_3 FS_i + \beta_4 IR_i + \beta_5 EXT_i + \beta_6 FIN_i + \beta_7 AFIC_i + \beta_8 L_{1i} + \beta_9 L_{2i} + \beta_{10} L_{3i} + Ui \quad \text{..............................} (5B.11)$$

$$Y_i^* = \beta_0 + \beta_1 SCWCS_i + \beta_2 FRSCCS_i + \beta_3 FS_i + \beta_4 IR_i + \beta_5 EXT_i + \beta_6 FIN_i + \beta_7 AFIC_i + \beta_8 L_{1i} + \beta_9 L_{2i} + \beta_{10} L_{3i} + U_i \quad \text{..............................} (5B.12)$$

Where, U_is are the random disturbances which are assumed to be normally distributed with zero mean.

The observed dependent variable Y_i is linked to the latent variable Y_i^* as per the following formulation:

$$\begin{aligned} Y_i &= 0 \text{ for } Y_i^* < 0 \\ &= Y_i^* \text{ for } Y_i^* \geq 0 \end{aligned}$$

INCOME GENERATED

The dependent variable in the present context is not necessarily bounded by any values. Further, we do not see any cluster of observations at or around any value. Hence, a linear functional form will be adequate in the present context. Thus, the three formulations of the regression model with linear functional specification to be estimated are as follows.

$$Y_i = \beta_0 + \beta_1 LI_i + \beta_2 FS_i + \beta_3 IR_i + \beta_4 FIN_i + \beta_5 L_{1i} + \beta_6 L_{2i} + \beta_7 L_{3i} + U_i \quad \text{............ (5B.13)}$$

$$Y_i = \beta_0 + \beta_1 SC_i + \beta_2 FR_i + \beta_3 FS_i + \beta_4 IR_i + \beta_5 FIN_i + \beta_6 L_{1i} + \beta_7 L_{2i} + \beta_8 L_{3i} + U_i \quad \text{................ (5B.14)}$$

$$Y_i = \beta_0 + \beta_1 SCWCS_i + \beta_2 FRSCCS_i + \beta_3 FS_i + \beta_4 IR_i + \beta_5 FIN_i + \beta_6 L_{1i} + \beta_7 L_{2i} + \beta_8 L_{3i} + U_i \quad \text{........... (5B.15)}$$

Where, U_is are the random disturbances which are assumed to be normally distributed with zero mean.

LABOUR INTENSITY

Since the dependent variable, that is, labour intensity, can take only positive value, the following exponential specification will be more suitable than the simple linear formulation.

$$Y_i = \exp(\beta_0 + \beta_1 LI_i + \beta_2 FL_i + \beta_3 AWP_i + \beta_4 L_{1i} + \beta_5 L_{2i} + \beta_6 L_{3i} + U_i) \quad \text{................ (5B.16)}$$

$$Y_i = \exp(\beta_0 + \beta_1 SC_i + \beta_2 FR_i + \beta_3 FL_i + \beta_4 AWP_i + \beta_5 L_{1i} + \beta_6 L_{2i} + \beta_7 L_{3i} + U_i) \quad \text{.......... (5B.17)}$$

$$Y_i = \exp(\beta_0 + \beta_1 SCWCS_i + \beta_2 FRSCCS_i + \beta_3 FL_i + \beta_4 AWP_i + \beta_5 L_{1i} + \beta_6 L_{2i} + \beta_7 L_{3i} + Ui) \quad \text{............... (5B.18)}$$

The above formulations of the regression model are non-linear in nature. However, by taking logarithm in both sides, we can make them linear and estimate easily. Thus, the final forms of the formulations of the model to be estimated are:

$$Ln\ Y_i = \beta_0 + \beta_1 LI_i + \beta_2 FL_i + \beta_3 AWP_i + \beta_4 L_{1i} + \beta_5 L_{2i} + \beta_6 L_{3i} + U_i \quad \text{........... (5B.19)}$$

$$\text{Ln } Y_i = \beta_0 + \beta_1 \text{ SC}_i + \beta_2\text{FR}_i + \beta_3 \text{ FL}_i + \beta_4 \text{ AWP}_i + \beta_5 L_{1i} + \beta_6 L_{2i} + \beta_7 L_{3i} + U_i \quad \text{.......... (5B.20)}$$

$$\text{Ln } Y_i = \beta_0 + \beta_1 \text{ SCWCS}_i + \beta_2 \text{ FRSCCS}_i + \beta_3 \text{ FL}_i + \beta_4 \text{ AWP}_i + \beta_5 L_{1i} + \beta_6 L_{2i} + \beta_7 L_{3i} + U_i \quad \text{.......... (5B.21)}$$

Where, U_is are the random disturbances which are assumed to be normally distributed with zero mean.

CAPITAL INTENSITY

Since the dependent variable, that is, capital intensity, can take only positive value, the following exponential specification will be more suitable than the simple linear formulation.

$$Y_i = \exp(\beta_0 + \beta_1 \text{ LI}_i + \beta_2 \text{ FS}_i + \beta_3 L_{1i} + \beta_4 L_{2i} + \beta_5 L_{3i} + U_i) \quad \text{.................. (5B.22)}$$

$$Y_i = \exp(\beta_0 + \beta_1 \text{ SC}_i + \beta_2\text{FR}_i + \beta_3 \text{ FS}_i + \beta_4 L_{1i} + \beta_5 L_{2i} + \beta_6 L_{3i} + U_i) \quad \text{.................. (5B.23)}$$

$$Y_i = \exp(\beta_0 + \beta_1 \text{ SCWCS}_i + \beta_2 \text{ FRSCCS}_i + \beta_3 \text{ FS}_i + \beta_4 L_{1i} + \beta_5 L_{2i} + \beta_6 L_{3i} + U_i) \quad \text{.................... (5B.24)}$$

The above formulations of the regression model are non-linear in nature. However, by taking logarithm in both sides, we can make them linear and estimate easily. Thus, the final forms of the formulations of the model to be estimated are:

$$\text{Ln } Y_i = \beta_0 + \beta_1 \text{ LI}_i + \beta_2 \text{ FS}_i + \beta_3 L_{1i} + \beta_4 L_{2i} + \beta_5 L_{3i} + U_i \quad \text{........................ (5B.25)}$$

$$\text{Ln } Y_i = \beta_0 + \beta_1 \text{ SC}_i + \beta_2\text{FR}_i + \beta_3 \text{ FS}_i + \beta_4 L_{1i} + \beta_5 L_{2i} + \beta_6 L_{3i} + U_i \quad \text{........................ (5B.26)}$$

$$\text{Ln } Y_i = \beta_0 + \beta_1 \text{ SCWCS}_i + \beta_2 \text{ FRSCCS}_i + \beta_3 \text{ FS}_i + \beta_4 L_{1i} + \beta_5 L_{2i} + \beta_6 L_{3i} + U_i \quad \text{.................................. (5B.27)}$$

Where, U_is are the random disturbances which are assumed to be normally distributed with zero mean.

6

Beyond Tenancy: Contemporary Agro-Economic Environment

Although the primary focus of the present study has been on the implications of tenancy relations for production efficiency and agricultural growth, the investigation was obviously carried out in a larger context of the overall agro-economic environment of the plains of Assam. As a result, besides the findings regarding tenancy and its impact, which have been presented and discussed in the preceding chapters, several aspects relating to the process of crop cultivation and the institutional economic environment surrounding the agriculture sector of the state have been observed. The discussion of the policy implications of the tenural situation of the state will be better accomplished if these important elements pertaining to changes and continuity in the agro-economic environment of Assam are also taken into account. Hence, the additional insights about the agro-economic environment of the state, gathered in the course of field investigations, have been briefly outlined in this chapter.

Development of Rental Markets

One recent development in the agriculture sector of the state, observed during the visit to the field, is the formation of markets for the services of many inputs of crop production. Among all such markets, the most crucial ones are those for the services of tractors/power tillers and, to some extent, of the bullock pair and instruments for irrigation.

During the field visit, it was observed that irrespective of the size of operational holding and tenure status, most of the farmers prefer to hire the services of a tractor or power tiller. We have come across many small and marginal tenant farmers who depend solely on the services of a tractor and power tiller for the preparation of land. Even those few farmers possessing bullock pairs prefer to have at least the first round of tilling done by a tractor or power tiller. Only a handful of farmers in the sample have tilled their land without the use of a tractor and power tiller.

What led to the emergence of these markets? Table 6.1 answers this question. The figures in Table 6.1 imply that there is a mismatch in resource endowments in terms of the ownership of capital goods across households. While not a single tenant farmer owned a tractor and power tiller, only a few relatively better-off (in terms of the size of operational holding) owner-operators possessed these capital goods. The mismatch in the endowment of capital goods means that there is scope for better allocation of these resources among rural households through transactions in the rental markets.[1] Consequently, rental markets for the services of these capital goods have emerged. It is interesting to note that such rental market transactions are profitable ventures for both the buyers and the suppliers of the services of these capital goods. While the buyers gain access to the services of these capital goods without having to own them, and thereby can overcome the resource constraints usually faced by the small farms, the sellers get to earn the rental income.

Table 6.1. Percentage Distribution of Sample Farmers Owning Capital Goods by Tenure Status

Tenure status	*Tractor*	*Power tiller*	*Bullock pair*
Pure tenants	0.00	0.00	33.33
Owner Operators*	1.62	10.27	55.68
Total	1.36	8.15	52.04

Note: * Includes owner operator-cum-tenant and owner operator-cum-lessor.
Source: Author.

Extent of Rental Markets for the Services of Inputs

Tables 6.2a, b, and c represent the extent of the rental markets for tractor/power tiller and bullock pair.

Table 6.2a. Percentage of Owner-operators Participating in Rental Markets for Tilling Equipment and Bullock Pair

Operational Holding (hectare)	*Tractor + Power tiller*			*Bullock Pair*	
	Possessed	*Didn't use*	*Hired*	*Possessed*	*Didn't use*
0–1	0.00	27.16	72.84	59.26	32.10
1–2	6.12	12.24	81.63	69.39	22.45
2–3	23.33	3.33	76.67	46.67	43.33
3–4	27.27	0.00	81.82	45.45	54.55
4–5	66.67	0.00	66.67	66.67	33.33
5–6	50.00	0.00	50.50	50.00	50.00

Source: Author.

Table 6.2b. Percentage of Sharecroppers Participating in Rental Markets for Tilling Equipment and Bullock Pair

Operational Holding (hectare)	*Tractor + Power tiller*			*Bullock Pair*	
	Possessed	*Didn't use*	*Hired*	*Possessed*	*Didn't use*
0–1	0.00	36.96	63.04	60.87	28.26
1–2	0.00	23.53	76.47	64.71	29.41
2–3	0.00	25.00	75.00	100.00	0.00
3–4	0.00	0.00	100.00	100.00	0.00

Source: Author.

Table 6.2c. Percentage of Fixed Rent Tenants Participating in Rental Markets for Tilling Equipment and Bullock Pair

Operational Holding (hectare)	*Tractor + Power tiller*			*Bullock Pair*	
	Possessed	*Didn't use*	*Hired*	*Possessed*	*Didn't use*
0–1	0.00	12.12	87.88	36.36	57.57
1–2	0.00	23.08	76.92	38.46	61.54
2–3	0.00	0.00	100.00	100.00	0.00
3–4	0.00	0.00	100.00	0.00	100.00

Source: Author.

It is clear from Tables 6.2a–c that while only a small proportion of farmers in the lower size classes did not use a tractor/power tiller, a substantially higher proportion of farmers hired the services of tractor/power tiller in all the size classes. This is true irrespective of the tenure status of the farmers. In fact, 100 per cent of the sharecroppers and fixed rent tenants in the relatively higher size classes hired the services of tractor/power tiller.

Insofar as the market for the services of bullock pair is concerned, given the greater extent of the market for the services of tractor and power tiller, it is obvious that the percentage of farmers hiring the services of bullock pair is not very high. Besides, a sizeable proportion of farmers across tenure status and size classes (except the fixed rent tenants in the size class of 3–4 hectares) owned a bullock pair. Nonetheless, a small proportion of farmers, especially the owner-operators and sharecroppers in the lower size classes, did hire the services of a bullock pair for tilling land.

Alongside the development of the market for the services of tractor/power tiller and bullock pair, another market that has emerged prominently is that for the services of instruments of irrigation, or more precisely, for the service of pump-sets. This rental market is important, especially for the fixed rent tenants who cultivate mainly water-intensive crops like summer paddy and winter vegetables. Since the sharecroppers predominantly grow winter paddy, they do not require irrigation.[2] Winter paddy is the major crop for owner-operators as well, although they grow water-intensive crops like summer paddy and winter vegetables on some parts of their lands. However, most of the owner-operators who cultivate these crops own pump-sets. Only three of the owner-operators who did not own pump-sets were found to have hired the services of pump-sets; the rest of them used their own. While it makes sense for owner-operators to possess pump-sets since they have their own land, the same is not the case for the fixed rent tenants. It might not be possible to purchase a pump-set due to financial constraints; nor would it be viable to purchase it, given the small scale of operation of the fixed rent tenants. Thus, they depend on the market for the services of the pump-set. Except for one, all fixed rent tenants were found to have hired the services of pump-sets.

In terms of the rent charged in the market for the services of tractor and power tiller, it has been found that although there are variations (see Table 6.3) across locations, within the same location (that is, in the villages of a district), the prevailing rent is the same. On the other hand, the usual arrangement across locations in the market for the services of pump-sets is such that a farmer pays 2–2.5 maunds (1 maund = 40 kg) of paddy to the owner of the pump-set while hiring it. Thus, if an absence of variations in price is considered an indication of the existence of a competitive market, the rental markets are competitive, at least locally.[3]

Table 6.3. Location-wise Average Rental Rate for One Round of Tilling (in Rupees/per bigha*)

Field Study Locations	*Tractor*	*Power Tiller*
Dibrugarh	113	188
Morigaon	213	163
Nalbari	98	113
Cachar	163	163

Note:* 1 bigha = 0.13387 hectare.
Source: Author.

The emergence of the market for pump-sets has an implication for the land lease market as well, due to the complementarities among markets for the inputs of production. As previously mentioned, in the presence of the market for pump-sets, farmers could cultivate the water-intensive crops which involve little production risk. Again, assured irrigation encourages farmers to use inputs like HYVs seeds, chemical fertilisers and pesticides, resulting in higher returns from these crops. Thus, higher returns and low weather risk have made the fixed rent tenancy contract the most preferred one for tenant farmers while leasing-in land to grow these crops.

CHANGES IN THE PROCESS OF CROP CULTIVATION

The implications of the market for the services of pump-sets are not limited to the land lease market alone. The emergence of a market for the services of irrigation instruments has enabled farmers to grow multiple crops. Farmers can now contract out most parts of the cultivation process instead of doing them themselves because of the emergence of the rental markets. All of these have implications for the labour market in terms of generation of employment.

The contracting out of different parts of the crop cultivation process and its implications require a little more elaboration. A decade or so ago, the process of cultivation was such that the farmer would stand behind the plough himself and perform each part of the cultivation process. S/he would, at best, hire labour to work alongside her/him during the time of transplantation and harvesting. But today, at least in those locations where the market for instruments of irrigation has developed, it has been observed that the way cultivation, especially that of paddy, is managed has undergone a sea change. Most farmers prefer to contract out almost all parts of the cultivation process. Starting from weeding to carrying the harvested paddy to the farmer's house, each part is contracted out. Contracting out is preferred by the farmers as it minimises the necessity to monitor to a large extent, which otherwise would have been a costly affair had the labour been hired on a wage contract.[4] Thus, the farmer's job has become less labour intensive; in fact, the farmer's role has been reduced to that of a manager. The farmer needs only to contract out the activity at the right time and occasionally supervise it.

The contracting out of different parts of the cultivation process has been possible due to the development of the markets for the various services required. For example, when a farmer hires the services of a bullock pair and tractor/power tiller, he does not use them himself to till the land. Rather, in some cases the owners of these items, and in most cases somebody appointed either by the owners of the tractor/power tiller or hired by the owner of the land, perform the job. Tables 6.4a–c show the extent of the phenomenon of outsourcing parts of the cultivation process, performed exclusively by human labour. It can be observed that the percentage of farmers who outsourced parts of the cultivation process is very high, and increases with the size of the operational holding. This implies that in the smaller size classes, more of family labour is employed, whereas the extent of outsourcing is greater in the higher size classes.

Table 6.4a. Extent of Outsourcing of Works Performed Only by Human Labour: The Case of Owner-operators

Operational holding (in hectare)	*% of farmers who outsourced parts of the cultivation process*
0–1	86.25
1–2	100
2–3	96.66
3–4	100
4–5	100
5–6	100

Source: Author.

Table 6.4b. Extent of Outsourcing of Works Performed Only by Human Labour: The Case of Sharecroppers

0–1	82.61
1–2	82.35
2–3	100
3–4	100

Source: Author.

Table 6.4c. Extent of Outsourcing of Works Performed Only by Human Labour: The Case of Fixed Rent Tenants

0–1	84.84
1–2	100
2–3	100
3–4	100

Notes: Outsourced works include transplanting, weeding, harvesting, and agricultural labour for the preparation of the field.
Source: Author.

Another interesting development that we came across in some places is the formation of groups of women workers to undertake the contracted-out parts of the cultivation process, especially to harvest the paddy field. Usually, one group consists of five to six women workers. The formation of such groups and the dynamics of their survival may be an issue worth exploring. But since this is not within the scope of the present study, we have not ventured into it and have left it for future research.

DISMAL STATE OF THE EXTENSION SERVICE

The agricultural extension service is supposed to bridge the gap between the agricultural research scientists and the farmers. It plays an important role in disseminating knowledge about the latest technological breakthrough in the crop cultivation process, seeds, and so on. Thus, the agricultural extension service is immensely important for stepping up agricultural productivity, and thereby the overall growth of the agriculture sector.

In the context of Assam, especially in all the locations of field investigation, it has been observed that the agricultural extension service is not very effective. The ineffectiveness of this service is already evident from the discussion presented in Chapter 5. Except for the proportion of area under HYVs seeds in the total rice acreage, the extension service has no significant influence on the other production and productivity enhancing practices.

During our field visit, we could realise from the farmers' responses that extension workers rarely visit the villages. None of the farmers interviewed said that the extension officer had visited the village during the past six months. As many as 84 farmers out of the 220 farmers surveyed did not even know who the village-level extension worker (VLEW) or gram sevak was in their locality. Only 43 of the remaining 136 farmers familiar with the gram sevak had consulted him. Although the VLEW was consulted, most of them did not follow his advice. Again, the majority of those few farmers who did follow the advice of the VLEW reported that it was of no use. The farmers are of the view that the suggestions of the extension workers are not practicable. For most of them, cultivation is a process of learning by doing; past experiences teach them what the right process of cultivation is. Thus, the gap between agricultural research and practice, especially in the context of the process of paddy cultivation, continues to persist.

One major objection, especially of the small and marginal farmers, against the extension workers is that they maintain contact only with the relatively large farmers. While the small farmers remain deprived of the benefits provided by the government, the large farmers appropriate all the benefits by virtue of their good contact with the extension workers. In fact, we have also observed that the farmers who spoke well of the extension workers were usually the ones who operate on a higher size of landholding.

Thus, from the above, it may be inferred that the agricultural extension service network in Assam is in a precarious state, and requires a major overhaul.

ABSENCE OF FARMER'S ORGANISATION

It has already been mentioned that not all farmers, especially not the small and marginal farmers, have a good opinion of the extension service. The small and marginal farmers alleged that extension workers maintained contact only with the large farmers. In fact, the small and marginal farmers complained to us that they were deprived of the benefits from other government schemes as well, especially in the case of the scheme distributing subsidised shallow tube-wells. According to many small and marginal farmers, the beneficiaries of such schemes are usually the large farmers and those who have contacts with the officials. In spite of the alleged discrimination against them, these farmers have to remain mute spectators since a small or marginal farmer individually is too insignificant to raise his voice. Had they been organised through an institution, they could have protested the alleged injustice meted out to them. But unfortunately, the small and marginal farmers are largely unorganised.

Field Management Committees (FMCs) are an institution that had a significant potential to uplift the conditions of farmers, especially that of the small and marginal farmers. But unfortunately, the FMCs in Assam have largely failed to realise their potential. In fact, most FMCs have ceased to exist, and the ones that are apparently operating exist only on paper. Now, most FMCs are in such a state of disarray that the members do not meet even once in six months to review the functioning of the committees.

Of the total farmers interviewed for the purposes of the present study, only 19.55 per cent were members of the FMCs. Membership of the FMCs, however, has not changed their condition from those of the non-member farmers. One of the reasons for the FMCs having had no effective impact on the condition of the farmers is the alleged non-transparent manner in which the heads of the FMCs conduct their functions. Most members of the FMCs alleged that the heads of the committees had kept them in the dark about government schemes, and appropriated all benefits of such schemes for themselves. Thus, there is a sense of mistrust among the members, which has resulted in the breakdown of the FMCs. Not receiving any benefits from being part of the FMCs, many member farmers have now withdrawn their memberships.

INTERLOCKED FACTOR MARKETS

Among the four field study locations, instances of exploitative interlocked factor market transactions were found only in the Narshimpur block of the Barak Valley. In six out of nine such cases, the lessors provided credit to the tenants. The tenants had to pay the principal and interest in kind (in terms of paddy). The rate of interest in terms of the market value of paddy in those cases ranged from 60 per cent to 120 per cent. Thus, the land and the credit markets were interlocked. In the remaining three cases, the tenants had to plough the land cultivated by the lessors without receiving any remuneration. This is clearly a case in which the land and the labour markets are interlocked. It may be mentioned here that in all the above nine cases, the lessors took active part in deciding the amount of inputs to be applied on the leased-in land.

NOTES

1. Figures in Table 6.1 relate only to the owners of tractor/ power tiller among the respondents. There are, however, some more households in each village that are primarily engaged in non-farm activity but own a tractor and power tiller, and rent them out to farm households in the village.

2. Winter paddy is sown during the summer and harvested during winter. Since it is sown during the summer, that is, the rainy season, it does not require irrigation.

3. So far, the government has played no role in regulating these markets. In fact, there is no need for government regulation since these markets seem to be competitive, at least locally. In a community set-up where everybody knows everybody else, it is difficult for owners of the agricultural machineries to discriminate among the buyers of the services of these machineries.

4. If the farmer had hired labour, s/he would have had to monitor the work of the labourer in order to ensure that the latter worked in the farmer's interest. However, when the job is outsourced, the farmer does not have to do the continuous monitoring. The arrangement is such that once the job is done, the farmer pays the person/party after ensuring that the job has been done to his satisfaction. If he is not satisfied, he may request the concerned party to do what is required before the payment is made. For example, in many of the villages it was observed that there were groups of women who did the weeding job. A farmer would outsource the weeding part of the cultivation process to one of these groups. The group informs the farmer once the job is done. The farmer then checks to see if the job has been performed properly. If he finds that more work remains to be done, he can request the concerned party to do so. The farmer makes the payment only after the group performs the remaining work.

Under a hired labour contract, the farmer has to pay the labourer on a per day basis. On the other hand, when the job is outsourced, the farmer pays only for the job, irrespective of the days taken to finish it. Given the arrangement or terms of outsourcing, it is thus in the interest of the party who takes on the outsourced job to work without shirking from the beginning so as to finish within the minimum possible time.

7

Conclusion and Policy Implications

The incidence of tenancy is extensive in the rural agrarian economy of Assam. Almost half of the farmers in the sample of the present study, covering four different agro-climatic zones of Assam, are fully or partially tenant farmers, and around one-third of the sample area is under lease. It has been found that all the tenancy contracts are informal, reflecting the fact that concealed tenancy is rampant in Assam. The fact that all the tenancy contracts are informal implies that the existing tenancy law has become redundant. This law, formulated against the backdrop of the agrarian relations prevailing at the time of Independence, primarily sought to safeguard the interests of tenants. However, since the tenancy contracts are not recorded, tenants cannot take recourse to the law even if they need to safeguard their interests. Although the law could not fulfil its objectives as envisaged, consequent to the strict provisions of the law, many unwarranted outcomes have surfaced. One such undesired outcome is the shortening of the duration of tenancy contracts. In the context of the present study, more than 60 per cent of the sharecropping and fixed rent contracts were found to be for less than three years. The short duration of the contracts has an adverse implication for the sustainable use of land. The tenants may not be interested in undertaking any investment into the development of the land. Besides, they may have no incentive to use the land sustainably. Rather, they may only be interested in maximising the returns from land during the stipulated short period by making excessive use of chemical fertilisers and such inputs, without caring to conserve the natural quality of the land. This tendency may be particularly strong among the fixed rent tenants as, after paying the rent, the only objective that they have is to maximise the returns from land. The present study has in fact found that fixed rent tenants tend to use more chemical fertilisers relative to the farmers operating under shareholder contractual arrangements.

In terms of the forms of tenancy contracts, the present study has found that sharecropping and fixed rent are the major forms of tenancy contracts prevailing in Assam. Again, between fixed rent and sharecropping, sharecropping is predominant in terms of number of holdings and area under this contract. Sharecropping exists largely in those locations where the principal crop grown is winter paddy. Winter paddy involves weather risk and sharecropping being a contract which shares not only the output, but also the risk associated with the crop, the tenants prefer sharecropping when they grow winter paddy. By contrast, crops like summer paddy, vegetables, and rape and mustard, which are largely grown on a commercial basis, involve little weather risk. Besides inputs like chemical fertilisers and pesticides, HYV seeds and irrigation are inevitably applied while growing these crops. The application of these inputs minimises the production risk caused by factors other than weather and fetches higher returns. Production risk being lower and returns being higher, tenants like to lease-in land under a fixed rent contract while growing these crops so that, after paying the rent, they can retain the entire return. On the other hand, even though lessors are able to overcome the information problem to a large extent, they continue to prefer sharecropping to wage contract as this allows them to release their managerial resources from the farm sector and devote them to the non-farm sector. Thus, it can be concluded that sharecropping contracts are more often the manifestation of attempts to manage risk by the tenant farmers, rather than the information problem of the lessor.

Insofar as the household decision to either lease-in or lease-out land is concerned, the availability of farm labour, level of education of the head of the household, and primary occupation of the household are found to have a significant influence on such decisions. While households with more labour tend to lease-in land, education creates an aversion towards agriculture and people with a higher level of education tend to lease out. Again, with respect to occupation, a household that is primarily engaged in non-farm employment chooses to lease out, as that enables a better utilisation of labour and other household resources in the non-farm sector. All these findings imply that tenancy is a pragmatic outcome of the mismatch between ownership of factors like land and labour. Those households which have more farm labour relative to cultivable land lease-in from those households that do not have sufficient farm labour. One important implication of the above findings is that as the level of education improves in times to come, and if more non-farm employment opportunities are generated through the proper implementation of programmes for rural development, there will be a greater supply of land in the lease market in the future.

The tenancy contracts have significant implications for efficiency in agricultural production and the sustainable use of agricultural land, and hence, for the overall agricultural growth. With regard to the debate relating to the relative efficiency/inefficiency of tenancy contracts, the present study provides proof to support the Marshallian argument, that is, that sharecroppers are relatively inefficient. The results of our econometric analysis show that tenancy in general and sharecropping in particular, especially sharecropping without cost sharing, have a negative and significant impact on production and productivity enhancing practices of cropping intensity, crop diversification, and the generation of income per hectare of operational holding and labour (input) intensity. On the other hand, it has been found that fixed rent tenants tend to devote a larger proportion of the rice acreage to growing HYVs and apply chemical fertilisers more than even the owner-operators. In fact, as the study shows, in the case of certain crops, the application of chemical fertilisers by fixed rent tenants is too excessive. As discussed above, the application of chemical fertilisers in liberal doses may have adverse implications for the sustainable use of agricultural land.

POLICY IMPLICATIONS OF THE FINDINGS

Before policy measures are suggested, one point requires reiteration. One has to understand that tenancy is a pragmatic outcome of the mismatch in the factor markets. Many studies have shown this earlier and the present study also validates it. Hence, it will not be prudent to attempt to suppress tenancy.

In view of the expected increase in the supply of land in the lease market (as discussed above), the main challenge of policy in this regard will be to ensure the efficient and equitable utilisation of these lands. In other words, while on the one hand the policy should ensure the efficient utilisation of the land, the farmers' access to land, on the other hand, should also improve. However, the present institutional set-up, or more precisely, the legislative measure, does not help to accomplish these objectives.

In order to protect tenants from the exploitation of the landlords and provide them with incentives by giving them security of tenure and conferring ownership rights upon them, the existing tenancy law in the state of Assam incorporated certain restrictive provisions. As per the provisions of this law, a tenant may become an occupancy tenant if s/he holds the land for three years continuously, and thus may consequently take over the possession of the land. In other words, the existing law does not distinguish between the use right and ownership right of land. These stringent provisions have instilled a sense of fear in the minds of the lessors, consequent to which many unwarranted outcomes have surfaced. Informal tenancy is one such undesired outcome. The lessors do not want the tenancy contracts to be recorded since they may create trouble for them later. If tenancy contracts are recorded and if the tenant holds the land for three consecutive years, the lessors may lose the ownership right. Thus, fearful of losing the ownership right, the lessors have forced informal tenancy upon the tenants. Since the tenancy contracts are not recorded, the tenants cannot take recourse to the law if they need to safeguard their interests. It is in this sense that the existing tenancy law has become redundant. Another unwarranted outcome of the tenancy law is the shortening of the duration of tenancy contracts. Even though tenancy is informal, consequent to the provision of a tenant becoming an occupancy tenant and then finally the owner of the land (should s/he hold the land for three consecutive years), the lessors prefer to lease out land for a short duration, usually for less than three years. As has been mentioned above, in the context of the present study, it has been found that more than 60 per cent of tenancy contracts are for less than three years. The adverse implications of the short duration of tenancy contracts for the development and sustainability of agriculture, especially in the context of fixed rent contracts, has already been discussed above. Thus, in view of what has been discussed above, one may question the effectiveness and necessity of sticking to the existing law in its present form.

Besides, one should keep in mind the fact that the context in which the existing law was formulated has undergone considerable changes over time. Therefore, the question that needs to be asked is: Are all the provisions in the law still relevant in the present context? Given the characteristics of landlords of the time when the law was formulated, the provisions of the law could have been justified. Today, however, there is evidence to suggest that the characteristics of lessors of the present time are different from those of landlords of the pre-independence period. In the context of the present study, it has been found that the lessors are not much different from the lessees in terms of landholding. There is not a single lessor in the sample of farmers in the present study who own more than 6 hectares of farm land. In other words, the lessors are also small and marginal, or, at best, medium landholders. Hence, protecting the interests of the lessors is as important as safeguarding the interests of the lessees. Taking away land from the lessors to transfer to the lessees will merely create another class of landless people. Another point about the changing characteristics of the lessors which deserves mention is that unlike the landlords of earlier times, lessors today do take an interest in agriculture. This fact is evident from the findings of the present study, which show that lessors monitor the activities of the sharecroppers and that many of them share some part, however small this may be, of the costs of cultivation with them. Therefore, it will be wrong to consider the present-day lessors as synonymous with the landlords of the 1950s or 1960s, whose interests lay not in agriculture, but in exploiting the tenants. All of these point to the fact that the existing law, or at least some provisions of it, may not be very relevant now.

Thus, in view of the changes that have taken place over time and the harmful effects of the existing tenancy law, reforms in these laws are warranted. In order to overcome the problem of shortening of the duration of the tenancy contract and to achieve the twin objectives of efficiency and equity in land utilisation, reforms which facilitate the leasing-in and leasing-out of land freely should be introduced. This calls for the scrapping of all restrictive provisions in the existing law, which in turn would mean distinguishing use right from ownership right. Distinguishing between use and ownership rights would mean that while the lessors would have the ownership right, the lessees would have the use right. This will allow the owner of the land to lease out for a considerably lengthy period of time without fear of losing the ownership right. If land can be leased-in for a lengthy period of time, that is, if the lessees have security of tenure, they may have the incentive to invest in the development of the land and also to use the land sustainably. Thus, the problems arising from the short duration of tenancy contracts may be avoided, and thereby the efficient utilisation of the land that comes to the lease market will be ensured. Further, the objective of the equitable use of land may also be accomplished as the tenant's access to land will improve if lessors do not hesitate to lease out land.

At this juncture, one point with respect to the duration of contract requires a little more discussion. While facilitating long-term leases may ensure the efficient utilisation and equitable use of land in terms of improved access to land for the present generation of tenants, it may hamper the attainment of inter-generational equity, as has been the case with 'Operation Barga' in West Bengal. If the present generation of tenants gets the right to cultivate land for too long a period, potential tenants may find it exceedingly difficult to lease-in. Therefore, the duration of tenancy contracts will have to be such that it provides incentives to the tenants to use the land efficiently, but at the same time does not make leasing-in very difficult for potential tenants. Thus, the biggest challenge involved in reforming the existing tenancy law centres round the fixing of the maximum duration of the tenancy contracts.

In addition to the above implications for efficiency and equity in the utilisation of land, distinguishing the use right and ownership right will have another equity implication with respect to the protection of the interests of the lessees. If the lessors can lease out without fear of losing the ownership right, they may not resist the recording of the tenancy contracts. If recording of the tenancy contracts becomes possible, it will allow the tenants to avail of the benefits of the tenancy law, especially with respect to protection against whimsical eviction by lessors and the payment of higher rent. The suggested policy measures, or more precisely, the reforms in the existing tenancy law, may take care of the above problems by taking into account the interests of both lessees and lessors. However, if we continue with the present provisions of the law, neither efficiency nor equity will be achieved. The stringent provisions may restrict the supply of land and land may remain unutilised. For fear of losing the ownership of land, the landowner may either keep the land idle or stick to agriculture even if it is not viable, which will restrict their occupational mobility. Such a situation is not warranted from the efficiency point of view. Besides, the tenant's access to land will get restricted if lands are not supplied in the lease market. Thus, the objective of the equitable use of land will also remain unfulfilled.

The reform measures suggested above should allow the land lease market to function smoothly. In view of the observed emergence of markets for the services of inputs of agricultural production (that is, the rental market), especially for the services of the power tiller, tractor and pump-set, facilitating the functioning of the land lease market will be immensely important to realise the full potential of the virtuous circle of market development. As discussed in Chapter 6, the emergence of the service market for irrigation equipment has positive implications for the labour and land lease markets. In those places where the market for the services of irrigation equipment has emerged, farmers have been able to cultivate those crops that involve less weather risk, but fetch higher returns. Consequently, fixed rent has been the preferred choice of contract in those locations. However, if the suggested reforms measures are not implemented, that is, if the farmers find it difficult to lease-in land for a considerably long period of time, the virtuous cycle of market development will not realise its potential, or may even collapse after some point in time. Since the fixed rent tenants tend to use more chemical fertilisers in order to maximise returns from land during the short period of contract, the result of this practice would be that after some time, the soil quality may degrade, and nobody would want to lease-in such land. Thus, the land lease market in these locations may break down, with adverse spillover effects on the markets for the services of other inputs of production. In other words, the virtuous cycle of market development may turn into a vicious cycle of market breakdown.

Finally, as has been observed, the emergence of the market for the service of irrigation equipment has positive implications for the land lease market in terms of choice of contract, and therefore for the overall development of agriculture. Alongside the reforms in the tenancy law, the development of irrigation infrastructure is also warranted. The importance of irrigation for agricultural development requires no explanation. In the context of the present study, it has been found that irrigation has a positive impact on all the production and productivity enhancing practices. Hence, along with the institutional reforms, the development of infrastructure for irrigation should also receive appropriate attention. A synergy between the suggested institutional reforms and the development of infrastructure for irrigation will lead to a better realisation of the agricultural potential of Assam. Initiative towards this end, however, can come only from the state. If the state takes necessary strides to develop infrastructure and put in place the required institutional reforms, it can be expected that the agriculture sector in Assam will emerge from the present state of low performance and move on to the next phase of development.

Bibliography

Appu, P. S. 'Tenancy Reform in India', *Economic and Political Weekly* 10 (33/35), 1975, 1339–75.

Assam Agricultural University. *Package of Practices for Rabi Crops of Assam*, Prepared jointly with the Department of Agriculture, Government of Assam, 2009a.

———. *Package of Practices for Horticultural Crops of Assam*, Prepared jointly with the Department of Agriculture, Government of Assam, 2009b.

Banerjee, A. V., P. J. Gertler, and M. Ghatak. 'Empowerment and Efficiency: Tenancy Reform in West Bengal', *Journal of Political Economy* 110 (2), 2002, 239–80.

Bardhan, P. K. 'Interlocking Factor Market and Agrarian Development: A Review of Issues', *Oxford Economic Papers* 32 (1), 1980, 82–98.

Bardhan, P. K. and T. N. Srinivasan. 'Cropsharing Tenancy in Agriculture: A Theoretical and Empirical Analysis', *American Economic Review* 61 (1), 1971, 48–64

Basu, K. 'Limited Liability and the Existence of Share Tenancy', in 'Collected Papers', *Theoretical Economics, Vol. 1: Development, Markets and Institutions* (New Delhi: Oxford University Press, 2005), 192–207.

Bell, C. 'Alternative Theories of Sharecropping: Some Tests using Evidences from Northeast India', *Journal of Development Studies* 13 (4), 1977, 317–46.

Bell, C. and P. Zusman. 'A Bargaining Theoretic Approach to Crop Sharing Contracts', *American Economic Review* 66 (4), 1976, 578–88.

Bezbaruah, M. P. *Technological Transformation of Agriculture—A Study in Assam* (New Delhi: Mittal Publications, 1994).

Bezbaruah, M. P. and N. Roy. 'Factors Affecting Cropping Intensity and Use of Fertilisers and High-Yielding Variety Seeds in Barak Valley', *Indian Journal of Agricultural Economics* 57 (2), 2002, 169–79.

Bhaduri, A. 'Agricultural Backwardness under Semi-Feudalism', *Economic Journal* LXXXIII (1), 1973, 120–37.

Bharadwaj, K. and P. K. Das. 'Tenurial Conditions and Mode of Exploitation: A Study of Some Villages in Orissa', *Economic and Political Weekly* 10 (5–7), 1975a, 221–37.

Bharadwaj, K. and P. K. Das. 'Tenurial Conditions and Mode of Exploitation: A Study of Some Villages in Orissa—Further Notes', *Economic and Political Weekly* 10 (25–26), 1975b, A49–A55.

Bhaumik, S. K. *Tenancy Relations and Agrarian Development: A Study of West Bengal* (New Delhi: Sage Publications, 1993).

Birthal, P. S., A. K. Jha, P. K. Joshi, and D. K. Singh. 'Agricultural Diversification in North Eastern Region of India: Implications for Growth and Equity', *Indian Journal of Agricultural Economics* 61 (3), 2006.

Borgohain, R. *Politics of Land Reforms in Assam* (New Delhi: Reliance Publishing House, 1992), 8–9.

Byres, T. J. 'The Dialectic of India's Green Revolution', *South Asian Review* 5 (2), 1972, 99–116.

Chakravarty, A. and A. Rudra. 'Economic Effects of Tenancy: Some Negative Results', *Economic and Political Weekly* 13 (28), 1973, 1239–46.

Chandra, N. K. 'Farm Efficiency under Semi-Feudalism: A Critique of Marginalist Theorist and some Marxist Formulations', *Economic and Political Weekly* 9 (32–34), 1974, 1309–29.

Chandra, B., M. Mukherjee, and A. Mukherjee. *India After Independence: 1947–2000* (New Delhi: Penguin Books, 1999).

Chattopadhay, M. 'Relative Efficiency of Owner and Tenant Cultivation: A Case Study', *Economic and Political Weekly* 14 (39), 1979, A93–A96.

Chattopadhyay, M. and D. Sarkar. 'A New Look at the Old Bottle: A Study on Land Tenure and Farm Productivity', *Indian Journal of Labour Economics* 36 (2), 1997.

Chattopadhyay, M. and A. Sengupta. 'Tenancy Inefficiency: A Study Based on West Bengal Agriculture', *Economic and Political Weekly* 36 (5–6), 2001, 497–502.

Cheung, S. N. S. *The Theory of Share Tenancy* (Chicago: University of Chicago Press, 1969).

Das, J. N. 'Land, Land-Relations and Land Reforms in the Plains and Valleys of North-East India', in Atul Goswami (ed.), *Land Reforms and Peasant Movement* (Guwahati: Omsons Publications, 1986).

Dobbs, T. and P. Foster. 'Incentives to Invest in New Agricultural Inputs in North India', *Economic Development and Cultural Change* 21 (1), 1972, 101–17.

Dwivedi, H. and A. Rudra. 'Economic Effects of Tenancy: Some Further Negative Results', *Economic and Political Weekly* 8 (29), 1973, 1291–94.

Fukazawa, F. 'Agrarian Relations in Western India', in Dharma Kumar and T. Roychaudhari (eds), *The Cambridge Economic History of India* (Hyderabad: Orient Longman, 1982), 202–03.

Gautam, H. C. 'Agrarian Relations: A Study on Some Aspects of Land Tenancy System in Assam', *Indian Journal of Agricultural Economics* 50 (4), 1995, 682–87.

Ghatak, M. and S. Roy. 'Land Reform and Agricultural Productivity in India: A Review of the Evidence', *Oxford Review of Economic Policy* 23 (2), 2007, 252–69.

Goswami, A. 'Land Reforms in Assam: A Critical Review', in Atul Goswami (eds), *Land Reforms and Peasant Movement* (Guwahati: Omsons Publications, 1986).

Government of India. *The Third Five Year Plan* (New Delhi: Planning Commission, 1961).

———. *The Tenth Five Year Plan* (New Delhi: Planning Commission, 2002).

———. *Some Aspects of Operational Land Holdings in India*, NSS Report No. 492, 59th Round, National Sample Survey Organization, Ministry of Statistics, 2002–03.

———. *The Eleventh Five Year Plan*, Vol. 3 (New Delhi: Planning Commission, 2007).

———. *Household Ownership and Operational Holdings in India*, NSS Report No. 571, 70th Round, National Sample Survey Organization, Ministry of Statistics, 2013.

Government of Assam. *Statistical Handbook of Assam* (Guwahati: Directorate of Economics and Statistics, 2010).

———. *Economic Survey* (Guwahati: Directorate of Economics and Statistics, 2011–12).

———. *Statistical Handbook of Assam* (Guwahati: Directorate of Economics and Statistics, 2014).

———. *Economic Survey* (Guwahati: Directorate of Economics and Statistics, 2014–15).

Guha, Amalendu. *Medieval and Early Colonial Assam: Society, Polity and Economy* (Guwahati: Anwesha, 2015).

Gujarati, D. N. *Basic Econometrics* (New Delhi: McGraw-Hill, 2004).

Haque, T. *Impact of Tenancy Reforms on Productivity Improvement and Socio-Economic Status of Tenants* (New Delhi: National Centre for Agricultural Economics and Policy Research, 2001).

Haque, T. and A. S. Sirohi. *Agrarian Reforms and Institutional Changes in India* (New Delhi: Naurang Rai Concept Publishing Company, 1986).

Hayami, Y. *Development Economics: From the Poverty to the Wealth of Nations* (New Delhi: Oxford University Press, 2003).

Hayami, Y. and K. Otsuka. *The Economics of Contract Choice: An Agrarian Perspective* (Oxford: Clarendon Press, 1993).

Herring, R. J. 'Abolition of Landlordism in Kerala: A Redistribution of Privilege', *Economic and Political Weekly* 15 (26), 1980, A59–A61 + A63–A69.

———. *Land to the Tiller: The Political Economy of Agrarian Reform in South Asia* (New Haven, CT: Yale University Press, 1983).

Indian School of Social Sciences. *Survey on Agrarian Structure and Social Change in Selected Villages in Kerala* (Trivandrum: ISSS, 1976).

Islam, M. M. and B. N. Benerjee. *Tenancy and Resource Use Efficiency in Agriculture* (New Delhi: Mittal Publications, 1985).

Johnson, D. G. 'Resource Allocation under Share Contracts', *Journal of Political Economy* 58 (2), 1950, 111–23.

Junakar, P. N. 'Land Tenure and Indian Agricultural Productivity', *Journal of Development Studies* 13 (1), 1976, 42–60.

Laha, A. and P. K. Kuri. 'Rural Credit Market and the Extent of Tenancy: Micro Evidence from Rural West Bengal', *Indian Journal of Agricultural Economics* 66 (1), 2011, 76–87.

Kuri, P. K. 'Factor Market Imperfections and Explanation of Tenancy: Testing an Econometric Model using Evidence from Assam of North East India', *Indian Journal of Agricultural Economics* 58 (2), 2003, 234–45.

Lal Bahadur Shastri National Academy of Administration. *Land Reforms in Assam: An Empirical Study (1988–1991)* (Mussoorie: Land Reforms Unit, 1994).

Misra, S. K. and V. K. Puri. *Indian Economy* (New Delhi: Himalaya Publishing House, 2000).

Mukherjee, R. *The Dynamics of a Rural Society* (Berlin: Academic-verlag, 1957).

Nair, K. N. and V. Menon. 'Lease Farming in Kerala: Findings from Micro Level Studies', *Economic and Political Weekly* XLI (26), 2006, 2732–38.

National Centre for Agricultural Economics and Policy Research. *Impact of Tenancy Reforms on Production and Income Distribution—A Case Study of Operation Barga in West Bengal*, NCAP Annual Report 1995–96, Chapter III. Available at http://www.ncap.res.in/upload_files/annual_report/1995-96/chap3.htm#a (accessed 10 July 2012).

Narayana, D. and K. N. Nair. 'Tenancy in the Context of Irrigation Uncertainty: Role of the Leading Input in Shaping Institutions', *Economic and Political Weekly* 29 (39), 1994, A129–A133.

Newbery, D. M. G. 'Tenurial Obstacles to Innovation', *Journal of Development Studies*, 11 (4), 1975, 263–77.

———. 'Risk Sharing, Sharecropping and Uncertain Labour Markets', *The Review of Economic Studies* 44 (3), 1977, 585–94.

Oommen, M. A. *Land Reforms and Socio-Economic Change in Kerala* (Madras: The Christian Literature Society, 1971).

Pant, C. 'Tenant and Family Resources: A Model and Some Empirical Analysis', *Journal of Development Economics* 12 (27–39), 1983, 27–38.

Patel, S. J. *Agricultural Labourers in Modern India and Pakistan* (Bombay: Current Book House, 1952).

Phookan, U., K. Gogoi, and P. C. Neog. 'Agricultural Development in Assam: District Wise Study, 1950–51 to 1975–76', Adhoc Study No. 45, Agro-Economic Research Centre for Northeast Region, Assam Agriculture University, Jorhat, 1980.

Place, F. and K. Otsuka. 'Tenure, Agricultural Investment and Productivity in the Customary Tenure Sector in Malawi', *Economic and Cultural Change* 50 (1), 2001, 77–99.

Pope, R. D. and R. Prescott. 'Diversification in Relation to Farm Size and other Socioeconomic Characteristics', *American Journal of Agricultural Economics* 62 (3), 1980.

Ramachandran, V. K. 'A Note on the Sources of Official Data on Landholdings in Tamil Nadu', Data Series No. 1, Madras Institute of Development Studies, 1980.

Ramakumar, R. 'Magnitude and Terms of Agricultural Tenancy in India: A State wise Analysis of Changes in 1980s', *Indian Journal of Agricultural Economics* 55 (3), 2000, 337.

Rao, C. H. H. 'Uncertainty, Entrepreneurship and Sharecropping in India', *Journal of Political Economy* 79 (3), 1971, 578–95.

Ray, D. *Development Economics* (New Delhi: Oxford University Press, 1998).

Saikia, Arupjyoti. *A Century of Protests: Peasant Politics in Assam since 1900* (New Delhi: Routledge, 2014).

Shaban, A. R. 'Testing between Competing Models of Sharecropping', *Journal of Political Economy* 95 (5), 1987, 893–920.

Sharma, H. R. *Agrarian Relations in India: Patterns and Implications* (New Delhi: Har-Anand Publications, 1995), 1–79.

———. 'Tenancy Relations in Rural India: A Temporal and Cross Section Analysis', *Indian Journal of Agricultural Economics* 55 (3), 2000, 295–307.

———. 'Liberalising the Lease Market', *Economic and Political Weekly* 41 (8), 2006, 696–98.

Sharma, H. R., P. Mehta, and K. Mohapatra. 'Tenancy Relations and Productive/Allocative Efficiency: A Study in Orissa Agriculture', *Indian Journal of Agricultural Economics* 50 (4), 1995, 597–608.

Sharma, N. and J. Dreze. 'Tenancy', in Peter Lanjouw and Nicholas Stern (eds), *Economic Development in Palanpur over Five Decades* (New Delhi: Oxford University Press, 1998).

Stiglitz, J. E. 'Incentives and Risk Sharing in Sharecropping', *Review of Economic Studies* 41 (2), 1974, 219–25.

———. 'Information and the Change in the Paradigm in Economics', in M. Szenberg and R. Lall (eds), *New Frontiers in Economics* (New York: Cambridge University Press, 2004).

Stiglitz, J. E. and A. Weiss. 'Credit Rationing with Imperfect Information', *American Economic Review* 71 (3), 1981, 393–410.

Tripathy, R. N. *Tenancy and Efficiency of Farming in a Developing Economy* (New Delhi: Mittal Publications, 1985).

Vaidyanathan, A. *India's Agricultural Development in a Regional Perspective* (Calcutta: Centre for Studies in Social Sciences, 1986).

———. *Agricultural Growth in India: Role of Technology, Incentives and Institutions* (New Delhi: Oxford University Press, 2010).

Vyas, V. S. 'Tenancy in a Dynamic Setting', *Economic and Political Weekly*, Review of Agriculture, 26 (5), 1970, A73–A80.

Index

in terms of production, but also in terms of their acreage share in the total cropped area, as is evident from Table 3.3.

Rice being the most prominent crop in Assam, an analysis of the growth performance in terms of area under production and yield of rice has been undertaken and presented in Table 3.5. The growth rates have been estimated by fitting a semi-log trend equation to area under production, total production and yield of rice between 2004–05 and 2013–14. During the period under consideration, the growth rate of rice production was an impressive 6 per cent. While the growth rate of the area was only 1 per cent during the same period, the growth rates of yield for autumn rice, winter rice, and summer rice were 6 per cent, 4 per cent and 6 per cent, respectively. In other words, the growth of rice production between 2004–05 and 2013–14 was made possible by the increase in the yield of rice.

Table 3.5: Estimated CAGR of Area, Production, and Yield of Rice in Assam from 2004–05 to 2013–14

Area		1.00
Production		6.00
Yield	Autumn Rice	6.00
	Winter Rice	4.00
	Summer Rice	6.00

Source: Author's own calculations, based on data from the Economic Survey, Assam 2014–15.

[illegible]

[illegible]

As per the Agricultural Census [illegible], there were [illegible] operational holdings in Assam, and the average size of an operational holding was only 1.11 hectare. Besides, the overwhelming majority of farmers were small and marginal farmers. The NSS data also reveals a similar picture.